Life *in the* Covenant

Life *in the* Covenant

in Family, Church, and World

Wilbur Bruinsma

Printed in the United States of America

Scripture cited is taken from the King James (Authorized) Version.
Italics in Scripture quotations reflect the author's emphasis.

Cover design by Daniel van Straaten
Interior design by Katherine Lloyd, the DESK

Reformed Free Publishing Association
1894 Georgetown Center Drive
Jenison, Michigan 49428
616-457-5970
mail@rfpa.org
www.rfpa.org

ISBN 978-0-916206-46-8
Ebook ISBN 978-1-936054-45-9
LCCN 2022950141

Contents

Section Three
GOD'S COVENANT AND THE BELIEVER'S LIFE IN THE WORLD

Preface

The world around us is rapidly changing. This is not merely true of the rapid advances in technology and medicine. It is especially true in the sphere of modern values and morals. A believer from four generations ago would wonder aloud why God has allowed this present world to progress in sin as far as it has. I'm a believer from three generations ago. I lived during the sexual revolution of the 60s and 70s when children out of broken homes (the divorce rate skyrocketed after World War II) declared their liberty from the restrictions society had placed on sex. Sex was divorced from marriage to become a matter of recreation and fun (free love). In decades following, the consequence of illicit sexual relationships, that is, conception, was successfully dealt with: birth control, abortion, or the proud defiance of women who decided that being a single mother was empowering. This sinful attitude toward sex has changed our society today so drastically that people now identify themselves according to their sexual preference.

I have also lived to see the working through of other trends initiated by the sinful 60s. A revolution against authority began, as if the authority of parents, church, and state was inherently evil. The older generation is now considered irrelevant. The young generation is convinced that the generations gone by have only succeeded in ruining the world. The young now are wiser following a new and better way. Yet lawlessness prevails in society. Radical feminism has influenced both society and, sad to say, many in the church of today, so much so that husbands hardly dare to exercise headship in their own homes. The cry that "God is dead" has developed into a society that ignores, or worse, despises the commandments of God. Christianity and its impact on western civilization are now hated. Pagan religions are exalted while true Christianity is labeled as vindictive, bigoted, and narrow-minded.

Yes, the world is rapidly changing. But God's Word stands the same yesterday, today and forever. This is true because God and his Son never change. The Christian faith therefore remains the same. It is relevant for each new generation—never outdated or immaterial. God's Word establishes unchanging values that believers of the modern generation must follow in the same way as did their parents, grandparents, and great-grandparents. We today have so much to learn from the generations of believers that have been born and raised in the covenant. This is true because the covenant itself has much to say about our lives.

This prompted me to write this book. The truth of God's covenant with his people in Christ is a practical matter. It is not merely theological in character. I know there are theological debates in order to maintain the blessed truth regarding God's covenant with his elect people. All good. But perhaps in it all we forget how much the truth of God's covenant with us and with our children has to do *with life itself!* The holiness of the church is founded upon our relationship of friendship with God! The doctrine of the covenant, therefore, has many practical applications that affect our lives in the home, church and the world.

Early on in my ministry, while living with my family on the island of Jamaica far from the safety and comfort of our churches, I learned a deep appreciation for the truth of God's covenant. My wife and children were my constant companions almost everywhere I went. My wife was my closest advisor. My children climbed with me the paths that led to the churches. I learned how precious family is. At the same time, I reflected upon the gracious benefits of being born in the line of the generations of God's covenant. My family and I lived and labored among a people whose society and churches were truly void of the benefits of God's covenant—something we so often take for granted as God's people. Through my years in the ministry I have addressed many of the subjects pertaining to life in the family and church. Many who sat under my preaching might remember some of my sermons, others some of my writings in the *Standard Bearer*.

This book is also the fruit of my experience as a parent who, together with my wife, shared in the joys and sorrows of raising our children and has witnessed the struggles of our own children in establishing godly homes. More than ever the pressures of a godless world have infiltrated the church through the media. The world makes sure that its views on sex, parenting, and the church are "in our face," so to speak. But God's Word also has much to say on these subjects; and what it teaches us is diametrically opposed to that of the world. It is my prayer that believers will either learn or be reminded by what is written here of how our relationship with God dictates the way we live in this present world of sin. I hope especially it is of encouragement to the young people and families of the church. May zeal and dedication to the cause of Christ in this world not pass us by! May God grant us to live in all godliness and holiness in the home, the church and the world.

—

Introduction

God's Covenant: The Believer's Worldview

We live in the last days. The signs heralding Christ's second coming emerge more clearly as the time approaches. As God loosens his sovereign reins on sin, society becomes increasingly more anti-God, anti-Christ, and anti-Christian.

Scripture warns us that in these last days:

> 2. men shall be lovers of their own selves, covetous, boasters, proud, blasphemers, disobedient to parents, unthankful, unholy,
> 3. without natural affection, trucebreakers, false accusers, incontinent, fierce, despisers of those that are good,
> 4. traitors, heady, highminded, lovers of pleasures more than lovers of God;
> 5. having a form of godliness, but denying the power thereof. (2 Tim. 3:2–5)

This accurately describes our present society and world. Everything listed in this word of God is taking place right now.

We live in perilous times, times that are dangerous and troublesome for the church.

With the rise of technology, the worldview of a godless society is at our fingertips. Christians, young and old, carry the world with them in their pockets as a constant companion, distracting them from life and labor. The lawless media dangles its immorality and violence before our eyes as a desirable gemstone. Many in the church are captivated, almost hypnotized, by the entertainment, gossip, and commercials boldly displayed by those who hate God and his commandments.

That this has had devastating effects on the church of Christ and her members cannot be denied. Many in the church at large have "a form of godliness" but deny "the power thereof." *In the church* immorality abounds. *In the church* the foundations of the family are shaken. The church is threatened by heresy from within and increasing pressure from without. Many in the church have accepted the narcissistic, hedonistic worldview and lifestyle of the wicked.

To counteract—no, to overcome—this type of mindset that is making rapid inroads into the church, we need to reexamine our values. How do Christians in their individual lives, in their homes and families, and in the church flee the "lust of the flesh, and the lust of the eyes, and the pride of life" (1 John 2:16; cf. vv. 15–17), so glamorized by the world about them? By seeking refuge in our God, who by his grace, for Christ's sake, watches over us as the "apple of his eye." God alone is able to preserve us from Satan, who seeks to overthrow Christ's church. We flee, therefore, under the shadow of God's wings (Ps. 57:1). But notice: the *reason* God preserves us is that he is our God and we are his people.

God keeps his covenant with his people.

The truth of God's covenant gives believers solid direction in life. This truth comforts us in distress, encourages us in our battle against our enemies, and gives strength when we are weak. To combat the threatening influence of the world upon our homes and churches, we need to embrace the truth of God's covenant. We must develop and nurture a worldview rooted in God's covenant.

Now, I realize that for some readers this worldview may seem completely foreign. We have not been informed, much less taught, about God's covenant. What is this covenant I am called to embrace? For other readers who are of a Reformed tradition, the concept of God's covenant is not new or novel. However, for many who have a Reformed background, the truth of the covenant has become nothing more than an abstract doctrine, the intricacies of which are left for theologians to debate. The warmth and beauty of God's covenant has been forgotten. The zeal to live according to that covenant has waned. A truth that has influenced Reformed believers for generations is now fading, to be replaced by the secular, worldly ideology of our unbelieving society.

For those who are hearing of God's covenant for the first time, as well as those who have allowed it to slip from their conscious experience, we must consider briefly what the Bible teaches us about God's covenant.

God's covenant is that intimate relationship of love and fellowship God has chosen to share with his elect people in Christ. Imagine that! God Most High, transcendent above all creatures in his glory and might, the God who holds in his hands the deep places of the earth, who with his fingers established the moon and stars in their places, who directs all the creatures of his hands to fulfill his sovereign will and good pleasure—*that* God chose a certain people to share in his life of love and fellowship! Imagine sharing the life of God with him. Imagine being taken into the family and household of God, loved by him, cared for by him, protected by him.

Throughout the course of history, God has spoken the words of his covenant. To Abraham God said: "I will establish my covenant between me and thee and thy seed after thee in their generations for an everlasting covenant, to be a God unto thee, and to thy seed after thee" (Gen. 17:7). The words of God's law to the children of Israel in Leviticus 26:12 spoke of this relationship: "I will walk among you, and will be your God, and ye shall be my people." The prophets repeatedly spoke the words of this relationship between God and his people. In Ezekiel 37:27, God says: "My tabernacle also shall be with them: yea, I will be their God, and they shall be my people." In Jeremiah 30:22, he says: "Ye shall be my people, and I will be your God."

Nor does this bond of love between God and his people change for his saints in the New Testament. Jeremiah prophesied of God's covenant with his church after Christ. We read in Jeremiah 31:33, "This shall be the covenant that I will make with the house of Israel; after those days, saith the LORD, I will put my law in their inward parts, and write it in their hearts; and will be their God, and they shall be my people." We know that Jeremiah prophesied this of the New Testament church because the writer to the Hebrews applies these words to us in Hebrews 8:8–12. Likewise, God's covenant is clearly laid out for Christ's church and people today in 2 Corinthians 6:16, "Ye are the temple of the living God; as God hath said, I will dwell in them, and walk in them; and I will be their God, and they shall be my people."

God gives several different promises in connection with his covenant, but there is an outstanding promise that reveals the unbreakable character of this covenant. Repeatedly throughout Scripture God speaks this promise to his elect people: "I will never leave or forsake you" (e.g., Deut. 4:31; Josh. 1:5; Ps. 94:14; Heb. 13:5). This knowledge gives the Christian the courage and strength to confront the greatest troubles and afflictions in life! When we are hurting, God keeps us safe in his loving bosom. When our enemies seek to turn us from him, God keeps our feet from falling.

In order to make this relationship of fellowship between God and his people more tangible, Scripture employs various earthly relationships to describe it. God speaks of a relationship of friendship that exists between himself and his elect people in Christ. He is their sovereign Friend who in his love, mercy, and grace shares the secret of his covenant with them. God speaks of his covenant in terms of a marriage and the husband/wife relationship. God in Christ is the Bridegroom and his church the bride. They dwell together in an intimate union, sharing in a blessed life with one another. Scripture also describes God's covenant as a parent/child relationship. God is our heavenly Father and we are his children, adopted in the blood of our Savior, beneficiaries of the blessings of salvation and the riches of heaven. As a Father, God dwells with his children in love, nurturing and protecting them.

Beautiful! Whether we are discovering the truth of God's covenant for the first time or being refreshed in it, we cannot help but behold the beauty and warmth of our personal relationship with the most high God! To the believer, this relationship is not some cold, abstract theological dogma he examines at arm's length, only to turn away untouched by what it teaches. This intimate relationship we share with almighty God becomes the warp and woof of our lives! Our lives in this world are inseparably woven together with that of our God! God's covenant becomes the fabric of life in the home, in the church, and in our place in this world. Living consciously and actively in the sphere of God's covenant, therefore, will directly influence our lives in all these spheres. Life with God determines how a believer views the world and his place in it.

What augments the beauty of God's covenant is what God himself reveals to us in establishing it with his people in Christ.

God's covenant is characterized, first of all, by God's love. The apostle John in his first letter focuses on this truth. This is especially in the foreground in 1 John 4:16, "And we have known and believed the love that God hath to us. God is love; and he that dwelleth in love dwelleth in God, and God in him."

That is a miracle! Why would God choose to dwell with us poor sinners in love and fellowship? The whole human race in the fall of Adam has alienated itself from God and his love and favor. We became the objects of God's wrath. We deserved punishment of the worst sort!

But this is where the amazing gift of God's love entered in! "God commendeth his love toward us, in that, while we were yet sinners, Christ died for us" (Rom. 5:8). Or again, "Herein is love, not that we loved God, but that he loved us, and sent his Son to be the propitiation for our sins" (1 John 4:10). God, in his great love and compassion toward his people, sent Christ into this world to restore us to his favor. We now dwell in communion with him.

This is why God's covenant is also a covenant of grace. We were not worthy of God's love and fellowship. We did not merit it in some way. God did not look at us and say, "Hmm, now I think that person is worthy of my dwelling with him. He has earned it." We are sinners. We were the enemies of God. We hated God and his commandments! But God, in his unmerited favor, powerfully delivered us from the horrible bondage of sin through Jesus Christ and graciously allowed us to dwell with him to experience his blessings and favor. By grace alone! A sovereign grace shown to his people in Christ.

In this God has also revealed his mercy. God's covenant is one of love, grace, *and* mercy. We all know how miserable sin is! It enters into the various relationships in life and seeks to ruin them. Sin as a wedge drives its way between husbands and wives, between parents and children, between members of the church, causing disruption and strife. How restless and weary we can become with the daily battle against sin! God, however, is merciful and speaks to us words of forgiveness, and therefore comfort and peace. He takes pity on us in our low estate, dragging us out of the mire of sin and making us partakers of his love and fellowship. Nor does God leave us in the mess sin makes in our life; instead, he renews our relationships with others through the cleansing blood of Christ.

With our salvation we are made to taste and see that God is good to us! His love, grace, and mercy are all very real to us! Nor can a person who shares in God's covenant blessings remain calloused to the reality that God and his Son sacrificed themselves that we might share in all this.

God's fellowship with us is a sacrificial relationship. God sent his only begotten Son, the Son of his love, to suffer eternal death for us. God poured out his fury on his *Son* for our sakes! Jesus said it: "For *God* so loved the world that he gave his only begotten Son" (John 3:16). That was the sacrifice God made in order to redeem us unto himself and restore to us the blessed fellowship we lost in the fall. And let's not forget the sacrifice Christ made. He gave his life unto eternal death in order to redeem us. This sacrificial, giving God now works in the hearts of those who have come to taste and see the beauty of

God's covenant. This mind of God and of Jesus Christ is now worked in those who share in fellowship with them.

My hope is that a little glimpse into God's covenant with his people will be enough to instill in us, by God's grace, a better appreciation for our relationship with God. If that is ours, we will, with heart and soul, sing the words of the Shepherd's Psalm:

The Lord my Shepherd holds me
Within his tender care,
And with his flock he folds me,
No want shall find me there.
In pastures green he feeds me,
With plenty I am blest;
By quiet streams he leads me
And makes me safely rest.[1]

This relationship of God's covenant will live in our hearts, determining how we live in the home, the church, and the wicked world around us.

Just one more brief consideration before entering into the subject before us: We need to distinguish between God's covenant with his church as a whole and his covenant with individual believers. Do not misunderstand: we are not speaking here of two different covenants. There is only one covenant. We merely distinguish the covenant as God establishes it with his church as a body, on the one hand, and with the elect members who belong to the body of that church on the other.

When God spoke the words of his covenant to Abraham, he explained that he would be Abraham's God. God established his covenant with this individual saint, therefore. But God also explained to Abraham that he would enter into a covenant with Abraham's children

1 No. 55:1, in *The Psalter with Doctrinal Standards, Liturgy, Church Order, and added Chorale Section*, reprinted and revised edition of the 1912 United Presbyterian Psalter (Grand Rapids, MI: Wm. B. Eerdmans Publishing Co., 1927; rev. ed. 1995).

in their generations. God established his covenant with the generations of Abraham as a whole (organically).

The error made by many in Israel (and by many today) is taking this to mean that every one of Abraham's children shared in the blessed favor and fellowship of God's covenant. The Bible proves conclusively that this was not the case (Rom. 9:6–13).

Nevertheless, God established his covenant with the nation of Israel (Abraham's generations) as a whole. He called this nation his son (Ex. 4:22–23) because Christ was to be born out of Israel. God refers in other places to Israel as his bride or spouse (Ezek. 16:6–8; Ps. 45). God uses the same language when speaking of the church in the new dispensation of the covenant (Eph. 5:22–33; Rev. 21:9). This is true because the church of all ages is one in Christ! What was true of the church in the Old Testament is true of the church yet today!

Believers in their need have often turned to the comforting words of Isaiah 41:8–10,

> 8. But thou, Israel, art my servant, Jacob whom I have chosen, the seed of Abraham my friend.
> 9. Thou whom I have taken from the ends of the earth, and called thee from the chief men thereof, and said unto thee, Thou art my servant; I have chosen thee, and not cast thee away.
> 10. Fear thou not; for I am with thee: be not dismayed; for I am thy God: I will strengthen thee; yea, I will help thee; yea, I will uphold thee with the right hand of my righteousness.

These words of God's covenant are addressed to the church as a whole.

God shares his favor, love, and fellowship with the whole of his church as the body of Christ, made up of God's elect. God dwells in the midst of her; she shall not be moved (Ps. 46:5). Because this is true, God also dwells personally with every individual elect saint in that church. No, not with every member of the church institute, but with every member of the elect body of Christ.

God's Covenant: The Believer's Worldview

God shares the love and fellowship of his covenant with every believer. God addresses us as individual saints of the church. For example, in Romans 8:14–17 we read:

14. As many as are led by the Spirit of God, they are the sons of God.
15. For ye have not received the spirit of bondage again to fear; but ye have received the Spirit of adoption, whereby we cry, Abba, Father.
16. The Spirit itself beareth witness with our spirit, that we are the children of God:
17. and if children, then heirs; heirs of God, and joint-heirs with Christ; if so be that we suffer with him, that we may be also glorified together.

Every believer knows and is assured that God is not just the God of his church, but that this God is *his* God forever and ever.

We make this distinction in order to understand that the truth of God's covenant directs believers in the way we conduct our personal lives in the home and family, as well as our place together with God's saints in the church as a whole. That is the focus of this book. God's covenant must be the world and life view of every believer. This worldview will in turn determine the way we conduct our lives in our families and the church, and as we live in the midst of a wicked world.

- Section One -

God's Covenant and the Family

—

Chapter 1

Setting the Solitary in Families

The family is precious to believers! The only other possession more precious is salvation.

But then, our sinful society also proudly proclaims that the family is important. In fact, our society quickly blames the Christian for being far too narrow-minded when it comes to defining the family. To the unbelieving mind, the family must no longer be defined in the conventional way.

According to the worldly "authorities," times have changed. The family unit may no longer be limited to a husband and wife together with their children. The concept of family, they insist, is much broader and embraces many different variations of the family unit. We may not exclude same-sex marriage and the adoption of children into such a relationship, or women who refuse to marry yet decide to raise children on their own. There are also families who, through multiple marriages, blend their children together into a new extended unit. There are families that consist of a man and woman living together outside of the marriage bond.

All of these, of course, are contrary to God's word and a violation of the seventh commandment. But the ungodly no longer view these relationships as sin and therefore, in their mind, the family includes all kinds of variations. Plus, the wicked angrily declare that any condemnation of these various forms of "families" is hateful and judgmental. Their conclusion? The family must not be all that precious to believers!

The pressure is on! This is not some distant concept from which the Christian church is immune. The *reality* expressed in this idea of the family is not just "out there" in society but is found already within the church. How are we to deal with this sinful new norm of the family, especially when it strikes near to home, among our own relatives and family members? How easy for us to succumb to the world's sinful view of the family.

The family as defined by Scripture is a creation of God. Nor was the creation of the family an arbitrary act of God in the creation of man and woman. The family unit is an expression of who God is. It is an expression of the life of covenant that is inherent in God himself. It may sound strange to say it, but God is in himself a family God! A trio of divine persons dwell together in perfect union and fellowship within the one being of God: the Father, Son, and Holy Spirit. One of the better books on the subject of the Trinity is authored by David J. Engelsma and is entitled *Trinity and Covenant: God as Holy Family*. In it, Prof. Engelsma develops the doctrine of the Trinity in a way rarely examined. He writes:

> He [God] is not the family God in the sense that this is a legitimate and helpful figure by which believers can know him, but in the sense that family is the nature of his being and the character of his life. God is the real family, the original family, the family after which "the whole family in heaven and earth is named" (Eph. 3:15). He is not the family God in some incidental way, but in a way that discloses the secret of the true, living God. Family is the meaning of the Trinity. This is the profound meaning of the Trinity that has been somewhat overlooked by the church in the West.[1]

The doctrine of the Trinity is not a cold, abstract dogma, best forgotten in the archives of ancient theological libraries. It is a living truth

---

1 David J. Engelsma, *Trinity and Covenant: God as Holy Family* (Jenison, MI: Reformed Free Publishing Association, 2006), 62

that has everything to do with our lives in this present world. Everything we believe, the very pattern of our lives in this world, is rooted in the God whom we serve. God's life within himself is essential for the lives of his people in relation to him.

That God is a family God is evident from the names of the persons within the Trinity: Father, Son, and Holy Spirit. Much of what we learn about the relationship between these persons lies on the edge of our human understanding since God is, after all, God—beyond all human comprehension. Yet, God reveals himself to us as Father. Why? Because as Father he begets the second person of the Trinity, the Son. God testifies to us that as God he is also Son. Why? Because as Son he is "the only begotten of the Father, full of grace and truth" (John 1:14).

The Father begets the Son; the Son is begotten by the Father. This is the language of Scripture. Now, it is not my intent to enter into any kind of explanation of this profound truth. There are books available that do that. It is my intent, however, to point out very simply the intimate life of love and fellowship shared between the first and second persons of the Trinity. They are Father and Son! The Son as the only begotten of the Father shines forth with the brightness of his Father and is the express image of the Father's person (Heb. 1:3). The Father and Son love each other with a pure and satisfying love within the very being of God. There is a relationship of friendship and fellowship that forms a bond of perfection, uniting these two persons into one. God is Father and Son!

What about the Holy Spirit? He too is a *person* of the Trinity who is active in the life within the being of God. We emphasize that the Spirit is a person because it is only a person who can share in the life of fellowship within God. The Spirit as a person belongs to the triune God as a member of the family. His name indicates his function in this relationship. He is Spirit who is breathed forth (proceeds) from the Father to the Son and who is, in turn, breathed forth (proceeds) from the Son back to the Father.

Once again, we can ask the question: do we understand this deep truth? No, not entirely! But this does teach us about the intimate relationship of love within the being of God. One of the Hebrew terms for "love" means to "breathe or long after." The double procession of the Spirit from Father to Son and from Son to Father seals the bond of love and fellowship between them.

All of this points to the truth that God is indeed a family God. This characterizes his very existence. God needs no one else outside of himself for love and fellowship. He has it all within himself. God did not create man because he was lonely and needed someone to share in a relationship of fellowship with him. God did not need our love. God enjoys within himself a life of joy unspeakable and full of glory. He is self-sufficient! God is a family God.

Yet, in eternity the triune God, according to his plan for all things, chose unto himself a certain people with whom he would share his life of love and fellowship. We learn in Ephesians 1:4–6 that God "hath chosen us in him [Christ] before the foundation of the world ... *having predestinated us unto the adoption of children* by Jesus Christ to himself, according to the good pleasure of his will, to the praise of the glory of his grace."

As we said, God was not compelled to do this on account of some deep need he had for someone to share in his life of fellowship. God chose to do this freely because it pleased him and in order to glorify himself. But notice: God, according to that eternal plan, elected his people *as his adopted children* in Christ. Before time began, before God laid the foundations of this earth, he chose us to belong to his family. We cannot fail to see the importance of the family to God. He is a family God, and in his eternal will for all things he chooses his people as his family.

When God created all things by the word of his power, the family did not simply occur as a byproduct of God's creation of the man and woman. The family is inherent in the very creation of the man and woman on the sixth day of the creation week. This is clear, first of all, from the creation account itself. On the sixth day of the week God created man out "of the dust of the ground and breathed into his nostrils the breath of life; and man became a living soul" (Gen. 2:7).

By virtue of his creation, man was a unique creature set apart from any other creature, including the animals. He had a mind and a will. But man was alone. God revealed that to Adam when giving Adam the task of naming the animals. As they passed before him to receive their names, Adam could not help but notice that God had created the animals male and female. Adam recognized that he was without a female counterpart. It was then that God caused a deep sleep to fall upon Adam. While he slept, God made out of one of Adam's ribs a woman. She was created out of his flesh and bone. Upon completion of the creation of the woman, God took her to Adam, and he immediately recognized her as his wife.

It was at this time that God instituted marriage. It is a creation ordinance. We know that because of the pronouncement made in Genesis 2:24, "Therefore shall a man leave his father and his mother, and shall cleave unto his wife: and they shall be one flesh." This is the beginning and foundation of the family unit: marriage. This is why David writes in Psalm 68:6, "God setteth the solitary in families." A man searches out a wife, and the two who were both "solitary" or single God now joins together into one, and they make up a family.

But God's intention in most instances is to add to this family unit. Adam and Eve received this command on the day of their creation in Genesis 1:28, "And God blessed them, and God said unto them, Be fruitful, and multiply, and replenish the earth, and subdue it." After God destroyed the world of men in the Flood, the same command came to Noah and his three sons and their wives in Genesis 9:1, "Be fruitful, and multiply, and replenish the earth."

God created man and woman in order that *within the marriage bond* they might procreate, that is, bring forth children. Children are a gift God grants to a husband and wife who live in love with each other in the bond of marriage (Ps. 127:3). When this occurs, that husband and his wife also become a father and mother. As their children grow up and mature into men and women themselves, the command is repeated to them to leave father and mother and cleave to a spouse to begin another family in their generation. So, the cycle is meant by God to continue from one generation to the next.

What then is a family? The Psalmist draws a beautiful picture of the family in Psalm 128:3, "Thy wife shall be as a fruitful vine by the sides of thine house: thy children like olive plants round about thy table." The family is made up of a husband and his wife who remain faithful to one another in marriage and, in their bond of love and fellowship, bring forth children in the fear of the Lord.

I know we must be careful when defining the family as such. Sometimes the Lord withholds children from a man and his wife. Certainly we would be wrong to say that the two of them are not a family. Again, at times the Lord forces a man or woman to raise children on their own because he takes from them their spouse, either in death or through sin. This too remains a family. Sometimes a man and his wife adopt children into their household. These children become part of a family. But all these instances are dictated by God himself. *God* withholds children; *God* sends death; *God* takes parents from children and then incorporates those children into a new family. God directs these affairs. But this does not alter the norm of a proper, biblical family: a man, his wife, and the children God has given them together.

What is redefined as family in today's wicked world is only the result of an unbridled violation of the seventh commandment. As soon as society gives vent to free, uninhibited, sexual lust, despising the limits God set upon the sexual bond to be used in marriage alone, it needs a new definition for the family. But all of this is an aberration of family.

To those who in faith enjoy the covenant God shares with them, the family is more valuable than all the wealth and pleasures this world has to offer. It is a manifestation of God's very own being, a revelation of his own divine life of fellowship! But more than that, God created the family because by means of it he chooses to share with that family *in their home* his life of love and fellowship. In the home we are given to taste and see that God is good. When a godly home is established, the triune God is present in the marriage and in the parent/child relationship. Together the members of that family enjoy the intimacy of God's presence as it overflows into the relationships in the home.

If only we can grasp the beauty of that in a small way! How important is your family to you? Husband? Wife? Parents? Young man and woman who desire to enter into the marriage bond, what effort are you willing to expend toward making your new family a place of fellowship with God and each other?

These questions need answering, of course. We will ask them again in later chapters. But first, we need to understand how important the family unit is and *why* God has placed the solitary in families.

Those who deny the family as the foundation of all society are like an ostrich with its head in the ground. The structure of the family determines the mindset of the various institutions of society, such as labor, government, the church, and the school. While dealing with an exposition of the fifth commandment, "Honor your father and your mother," Herman Hoeksema writes:

> And the family is the beginning, the basis, the root, of all the different relationships that exist and develop in the organism of the human race. From the home develops society and all the different relationships implied in that term. From the home also develops the institution of the state and all the different gradations of positions of authority which there are in the state as institution.[2]

In the home a child is first introduced to authority. When the child is left to himself in the home, never disciplined, or is coddled by parents who give in to every whim and wish of the child, he will grow up to be a law unto himself. He will be spoiled, thinking the world owes him everything. He will then carry this attitude into the workforce. It will shape his

2 Herman Hoeksema, *The Triple Knowledge*, 3 vols. (Jenison, MI: Reformed Free Publishing Association, 1972), 3:277.

view of government and of the church. When a child is properly trained, he will be a good citizen, a faithful laborer, and a productive member of the church. This has proven itself in generations come and gone.

Today we see a horrible breakdown of the family. Children are no longer taught chastity, temperance, and respect for authority in the home. Instead, domestic violence, abuse, and neglect pervade many families both in society and even in the church. This is why we see so much violence, immorality, and despising of authority in our society at large. With the collapse of the family comes the collapse of society. Yet the world still sings of peace and love when there is no peace and love. Our world is without Christ! This begins with one basic fact: *families* are without Christ!

But God has a more specific purpose in establishing the unit of the family. By means of the family God intends to perpetuate his covenant in the line of believers and their children. Ah yes! The covenant! The family God, the God of covenant, sets the solitary in families in order that the *believing* family might experience the beautiful life of God's covenant. But God also establishes the family in order that the fellowship of his covenant might be preserved in the line of their continued generations.

This blessing of home and family, of course, belongs only to those in whom God has worked by his grace. God's purpose regarding his covenant is very narrow. It is limited to his elect people whom he saves in Christ and unites to him in fellowship through the work of the Holy Spirit in their hearts. The majority of families in this wicked world (and even many within the church world at large) are not included in this purpose of God regarding the family.

God, according to his purpose, sets believers in families! A man united to Christ by a true and living faith seeks out a wife that is of the same faith. Once married, they establish a home where they bring forth children and, on the basis of God's promise that he will save in the line of generations, diligently nurture, discipline, and instruct their children in the fear of God. Again, by God's grace these children grow up and do the same.

The Psalmist in Psalm 78:5–7 explains this in simplest of terms:

5. For he [Jehovah] established a testimony in Jacob, and appointed a law in Israel, which he commanded our fathers, that they should make them known to their children:
6. that the generation to come might know them, even the children which should be born; who should arise and declare them to their children:
7. that they might set their hope in God, and not forget the works of God, but keep his commandments.

This simple instruction is so easily forgotten. The difficult, time-consuming task of believers whom God has set in families is to establish a home where Christ dwells, a home where everyone enjoys fellowship with each other, and especially where the greatest blessing is to know and love God together. "Behold, that thus shall the man be blessed that feareth the LORD. The LORD shall bless thee out of Zion: and thou shalt see the good of Jerusalem all the days of thy life. Yea, thou shalt see they children's children, and peace upon Israel" (Ps. 128:4–6). How does your family compare to this? This is the purpose of God in creating the family.

A second purpose of God is a bit broader but stands inseparably connected to preserving the line of believers from one generation to the next in believing families. It is also God's purpose to gather and preserve his church in the line of the generations of these believing families. God does not establish his covenant with a number of random, scattered families who have little to do with each other. God always saves his people in connection with his church in this world. Just as God sets solitary believers in families, so also God sets believing families in the church.

Assuming this is true, then it also follows that God uses godly families in order to preserve his church from generation to generation. In fact, good, solid families are indispensable for the preservation of Christ's church. A church made up in large part of families that hold little appreciation for God's covenant will eventually fall. Families that are concerned with only putting on an outward show for others while there is no peace within the walls of that household cannot form the basis of a strong and healthy church. Only that church filled with families that live out God's covenant, exercising themselves in godliness, will God preserve in the generation to come. When families fail, the church fails.

This is why Satan is relentless in his attacks against the family. There are times when the church battles against heresy as it creeps into the sphere of the church. Loud voices are raised in defense of orthodoxy. No doubt, Satan uses false doctrine to destroy the church of Jesus Christ too. The church must always be aware of this attack of Satan upon the church. But while the battle for orthodoxy is waged, Satan is busy on another front: the family. Satan is shrewd! While the church defends herself from error, Satan uses this battle to divert attention from a canker that can eat away at the heart of God's covenant with the church: the breakdown of the family. Satan takes delight in destroying marriages. He rubs his hands together with glee when he is able to drive a wedge between husbands and wives or parents and children.

Satan uses the influences of the world to achieve his grand design to destroy the covenant God has established with families. The media is an effective tool in his hand. Through the repeated efforts of the wicked world through the media of today, Satan rubs us until we become calloused to what the world thinks about family. Then, through more prodding, we even become sympathetic toward the views of the world. We begin to accept those who walk in open defiance against the word of God and what he explicitly teaches us about family. When we defy the biblical family, we defy God himself, because God is a family God! This is exactly what Satan seeks to achieve.

Pause for a moment and contemplate the beauty of a home that basks in God's fellowship and favor. What a precious gift he has given us in our families! Based on the knowledge of who God is and the life he has within himself, we need to strive all the more to make our homes a means through which God will carry on his church and covenant in our generations.

Chapter 2

The Covenant of Marriage

Marriage has fallen on hard times. It is generally agreed by those who determine such statistics that forty to fifty percent of first-time marriages end up in divorce or permanent separation. The reasons given by those who have divorced are myriad, including unrealistic expectations, lack of commitment, constant fighting, infidelity, lack of equality in the marriage, and getting married too young. The reasons given by those who have counseled people in such marriages are a little different. A life of fornication prior to marriage, including premarital cohabitation, precludes the need or desire to settle down into a permanent relationship in marriage. A lack of religious affiliation coincides with the divorce rate. The emancipation of women by means of the feminist movement has led to social and economic independence of a man and his wife, as well as strife regarding their callings in marriage.

The permanency of the marriage bond is disintegrating more rapidly as time goes on. Again, statistics reveal that the chance of divorce doubles when the parents of one of those marrying are divorced. They triple when both sets of parents of those marrying are divorced. Divorce perpetuates itself in the generations of those who divorce or permanently separate. This is not to say, of course, that the grace of God cannot break the cycle. It most certainly can and does! As Paul says in Romans 5:20, "But where sin abounded, grace did much more abound." But this does not diminish the astounding success Satan has achieved in destroying the family and the church. And it is increasing!

The wicked world, in its movies and songs, accepts and even glorifies a life of sexual debauchery and immorality outside of marriage. Divorce is viewed as normal—a fact of life. The younger generation of the church is bombarded with this hedonistic view of life on the television, computer, and, more recently, on the mobile phone.

What is the antidote against this poison of the world? Grace, of course! Salvation in Christ is the only means by which we are delivered from the darkness of sin and unbelief! Yet, due to the sinful flesh in us, believers too are capable of falling into the sins of this present world. To combat the world, we need to "draw near [to God] with a true heart in full assurance of faith, having our hearts sprinkled from an evil conscience, and our bodies washed with pure water" (Heb. 10:22). In faith we need to examine the relationship God through Christ has established with us and his church in this world. Doctrine and practice can never be separated. What God's word teaches us about God's covenant with us will certainly have a direct bearing on our marriages!

God has married his church!

God's word to Israel through the mouth of the prophet Jeremiah states it plainly: "Turn, O backsliding children, saith the LORD; *for I am married unto you*: and I will take you one of a city, and two of a family, and I will bring you to Zion" (3:14). One of the most beautiful passages of the Bible describing the work of God's grace in his church is in Ezekiel 16. Jehovah explains there that he delivered the nation of Israel from the filth of her sin and gave her life. As a result, she developed in beauty that was made perfect through God's comeliness. We then read in verse 8: "Now when I passed by thee, and looked upon thee, behold, thy time was the time of love; and I spread my skirt over thee, and covered thy nakedness: yea, I swear unto thee, and entered into a covenant with thee, saith the Lord GOD, and thou becamest mine."

The Covenant of Marriage

Because God reveals himself in Christ, the New Testament explains *Christ's* relationship to the church as that of marriage, too. Jesus spoke of himself as the bridegroom and the church as his bride: "And Jesus said unto them, Can the children of the bridechamber mourn, as long as the bridegroom is with them? but the days will come, when the bridegroom shall be taken from them, and then shall they fast" (Matt. 9:15). Paul compares earthly marriage to the marriage of Christ and his bride, the church, in Ephesians 5:31–32, "For this cause shall a man leave his father and mother, and shall be joined unto his wife, and they two shall be one flesh. This is a great mystery: but I speak concerning Christ and the church."

Scripture speaks of God's relationship with his church in Christ in terms of marriage for two reasons. First, the relationship of a husband and wife emphasizes the union or bond of God's covenant with his people in Christ. Second, marriage points to the relationship itself that exists between God and his church. An understanding of these will profoundly influence how a believing husband and wife view their marriage and behave towards one another in marriage. In this chapter we will treat the first of these reasons. We wish to focus on the bond of marriage.

God's covenant is a bond, just as is marriage. God, by his grace, not only accepts us into his presence and becomes our God so that we become his people, but he also takes to himself those who are unworthy, having merited nothing in his sight, and *binds* them to himself in the closest possible union. God accomplishes this through the work of our Savior in two ways.

First, God's covenant is a legal bond established with his elect people on the basis of Christ's righteousness. Through his suffering on the cross, Christ earned for his people the right to become God's bride. Certainly God would not be unequally yoked together with unbelievers. All men in Adam fell into the deep way of sin. We became guilty before God and worthy of judgment and death. We alienated ourselves from God's fellowship through the sin that is in us. In order for God to enter into covenant with us, he must deliver us from the guilt of our sin. We must be made righteous before God. Christ has accomplished this by means of our justification. Christ paid the price for sin, God imputed to us Christ's righteousness, and we now are worthy of sharing in God's fellowship.

On the basis of Christ's righteousness, God now takes his church, the body of elect believers, unto himself as his bride. He speaks to her the marriage vow: "I will not leave you or forsake you!" He seals his covenant with an oath. "Yea, I sware unto thee, and entered into a covenant with thee, saith the Lord God, and thou becamest mine" (Ezek. 16:8). God *legally* binds his church together with him in the blood of Jesus Christ, and the church becomes his royal bride.

Second, God binds elect believers unto himself in an organic union with Christ so that the church might become one body together with Jesus Christ. In a very real way *spiritually*, the church becomes flesh of Christ's flesh and bone of his bone (Eph. 5:30). This work of our Savior takes place through his Spirit. When Christ sends forth his Spirit to dwell in our hearts, that Spirit applies to us the blessings of salvation. The moment he takes up his dwelling place in our hearts, we are regenerated—brought from death into life.

At that moment too, we are grafted into our Lord Jesus Christ by a true and living faith. Grafting is the art of taking a branch cut from one tree and binding it together with the stock of another tree. As a result of this grafting, the life of the tree flows forth into the branch. The same is true with the work of the Spirit in our salvation. The Spirit grafts (binds) believers into Jesus Christ and the life of our Savior flows forth out of him and into us. We are bound to Christ in such a way that we become one with him. We are united to Christ, becoming one body with him. Such union with Christ leads to union with God himself. This is how, organically, the church becomes the bride of God in Christ and shares in the intimate fellowship of God's covenant.

The perceptive reader will already notice what this has to do with his or her own marriage. But before explaining this, one more truth concerning this relationship of God's covenant (marriage) is vital to our understanding of marriage: God's bond with his bride the church is *unbreakable*!

This claim rests, first of all, upon the oath God spoke when establishing his covenant. We learn in Hebrews 6:17–18 that

> 17. God, willing more abundantly to shew unto the heirs of promise the immutability of his counsel, confirmed it by an oath:
> 18. that by two immutable things, in which it was impossible for God to lie, we might have a strong consolation, who have fled for refuge to lay hold upon the hope set before us.

The unchangeable God of truth swears by his own name that he will be our God and dwell with us unto all eternity in his love and friendship. God will never swerve from that oath! He will not leave or forsake his bride the church because God does not change. God's oath to the church will never be broken.

The claim that God's covenant is unbreakable also rests on the truth that when grafted into Jesus Christ we become one flesh with him. We are the members of his body. We are *in* Christ and he *in* us. We are one with each other. That means nothing will separate us from the love of God which is in Christ Jesus our Lord. This is the beautiful and comforting truth of the preservation of the saints. God will never forsake his bride; he will never go back on his covenant and its promises.

The relationship of God's covenant now becomes the pattern for our marriages. Not the other way around. God does not use our marriages as a picture of Christ and the church. Believers' marriages are based upon and patterned after the intimate bond of God's covenant with his elect church.

This is why marriage must be rooted in a man and woman's relationship with God. To make a marriage strong Christ must dwell with a husband and wife in their home! For this reason, parents must teach their young men that when they seek a wife, they must find a woman who exhibits a love for God and a desire for his fellowship. Likewise, parents must teach their young women to accept a date only with a young man who has already exhibited faith in Jesus Christ and walks in the light. Parents may not neglect this instruction. Nor may they give in to the pleadings of their child when the child seeks to disobey this instruction.

It is not enough to teach our children and youth to find a spouse from one's own denomination of churches. This is a good thing to teach our children. It sets a marriage in good stead from the very start when a young man and woman believe the same truths of the Scripture. It is important that they seek one who believes the same way as they do. But that is not *enough*. Some who dwell within the sphere of God's covenant and church are not true believers. They are tares that may look like the wheat for a time but are deceivers. The truth of God's word stands out: "they are not all Israel that are of Israel."

What then must our sons and daughters look for in a man or woman they seek to marry? Faith! Not, "Do they go to the same church as I do?" We must teach our children to have discerning eyes. Does that young man, does that young woman know their sin? Do they seek and find forgiveness in the cross of Jesus Christ? Do they walk in humble gratitude before God? Are they interested in spiritual things? Are the fruits of faith evident in their works?

On the basis of their faith in God and his covenant, a man and woman establish a marriage that is itself a covenant. Yes, it is a bond into which a man and woman enter, but, in reality, it is a bond that God establishes. *God* joins a man and woman together in the covenant of marriage in order to reveal the covenant between himself and his bride, the church. This is the mystery of marriage. For the unbeliever this means nothing. But for the believer who has been drawn to God and enjoys the close communion of his covenant, this means everything! He views his marriage in an entirely different light!

When a man and his bride speak their vows to one another, they make their marriage legally binding. They speak those vows before

God and an assembly of God's people as their witnesses. "I take you to be my lawfully wedded wife (or husband) ... until death do us part." A vow is as binding as an oath. The difference is that a vow does not actually call upon the name of God as a witness as when one swears an oath. But a vow is a solemn pledge or promise that *assumes* that God is a witness to what is said. This makes a vow just as serious as an oath.

In his monumental work on the subject of divorce and remarriage, Andrew Cornes writes:

> But what if one or both of a couple makes a vow with mental reservations? What if they vow to "take you to be my wife/husband...till death us do part" but at the same time think "or until one of us can't stand the other anymore and we separate"? Numbers 30 makes it absolutely clear that all vows must be performed and that the Lord will not "release" a person from a vow even if it is a "rash promise" (Num. 30:6–8).[1]

Just like God's oath that he swears to his bride the church, "I will never leave you or forsake you," so also the vow that is made at the time of marriage, "Till death do us part," is legally binding upon those individuals entering into marriage. This is the seriousness of the vows taken at the time of the wedding ceremony. Marriage is not a quaint, romantic fairytale wedding with bride and groom ignoring the marriage form and speech because hearts are floating around their heads!

We can surround our weddings with all kinds of pomp and circumstance, but in the end something mysterious is taking place. *By means of the wedding and its vows, God is joining into one flesh a man and a woman.* They enter into a binding legal covenant with one another that must reflect God's covenant with his people. Marriage is a legal bond.

---

1 Andrew Cornes, *Divorce and Remarriage: Biblical Principles and Pastoral Practice* (Grand Rapids, MI: Eerdmans, 1993), 41.

And more, marriage is an organic bond between a husband and wife. By means of the wedding bed, a man and wife become one flesh with each other. God ties two people into one. God welds them together.

In a promiscuous age in which sex becomes recreational—a matter of fun—a young man and women need to take seriously that the sexual union is reserved for marriage. Those who walk in fornication are more likely to end up in divorce when they later marry.

The sexual union is not a toy. Casual sex outside of marriage is an abomination in the eyes of the God of the covenant! God uses this union to weld into one flesh a man and his wife. This is why Jesus allows divorce only on the ground of adultery in the marriage, so important is the sexual union between a man and his wife.

Of course, the idea of one flesh includes more than the sexual union. God binds a man and wife together physically, spiritually, and psychologically. They begin to function together as one. They may have their own individual opinions and ideas on matters, but these all converge and blend together with the thoughts and opinions of one's spouse. When sin enters into the relationship and causes division between the two it is painful and bitter. In these instances when separation or divorce occur, it is never cordial. This is true because man cannot divide what God has tied together.

When two believers enter into marriage it is with the firm conviction that, for better or worse, it is a lifelong bond—an unbreakable bond. What a shaky start to a marriage if this is not in the hearts of both the bridegroom and his bride when they speak their vows! Just as God's covenant with us in Christ is permanent, so also is marriage. How frustrating when the church makes a stand against unlawful divorce and remarriage—a stand which is indeed biblical—but then members of the church begin to circumvent this by searching out ways to divide a man and wife on grounds other than adultery. This looks at marriage from the wrong perspective!

We who are in Christ may not enter marriage with this negative perspective on our marriage: "We do not believe in unlawful divorce and remarriage." That is not what we believe. That is what we do *not* believe. Rather, this ought to be the outlook on our own marriage: "We believe in the permanency of marriage." Why? Because the believing husband and wife, together as one, live out of the life that God shares with them in Christ. When a married person seeks to dissolve this union in any way, his or her union with Christ comes into question.

The apostle Paul speaks of the permanency of marriage in Romans 7:2, "For the woman which hath a husband is bound by the law to her husband so long as he liveth; but if the husband be dead, she is loosed from the law of her husband." This, of course, has much to say about remarriage. Paul continues in verse 3: "So then if, while her husband liveth, she be married to another man, she shall be called an adulteress: but if her husband be dead, she is free from that law; so that she is no adulteress, though she be married to another man."

Paul emphasizes the permanency of marriage. Marriage ends for a wife upon the death of her husband. Likewise, marriage ends for a husband upon the death of his wife. It is important, however, to understand that this instruction ties in with what Paul teaches in Romans 7:4, "Wherefore, my brethren, ye also are become dead to the law by the body of Christ; that ye should be married to another, even to him who is raised from the dead, that we should bring forth fruit unto God." Notice how the permanency of marriage is tied together with our relationship to Christ. We were married to the law once, but we are now dead to the law through Christ's death on the cross. Because this is true, we are now married to Christ. That marriage relationship with Christ can never be broken, not even by death. Once again, God's word in this passage reveals how earthly marriage is a reflection of our union with Christ.

When this conviction dwells in our hearts, it will lead to a solid marriage. When I, as a young person, search in faith to marry someone who is convicted of God's covenant; when I, on my wedding night, speak my vows in faith before God, convinced of the permanency of marriage; when I in faith live out God's covenant with my spouse, God will bless my home with security and joy. God will bless my marriage. There will be nothing better on earth than that union of husband and wife! Why is this true? Because my spouse and I were, are, and always will be convicted that marriage is as permanent as Christ's relationship with us.

Chapter 3

Our Calling in Marriage

Scripture speaks not only of the *covenant* of marriage but also of the *relationship* of marriage that exists between Christ and his church. This reflects on the calling of husbands and wives in marriage. We mentioned that at the beginning of the last chapter. In this chapter, we wish to examine what God's covenant teaches us about how husbands and wives dwell with each other in marriage.

Ephesians 5:22–33 teaches us of the relationship between Christ and his wife, the church:

> 22. Wives, submit yourselves unto your own husbands, as unto the Lord.
> 23. For the husband is the head of the wife, even as Christ is the head of the church: and he is the saviour of the body.
> 24. Therefore as the church is subject unto Christ, so let the wives be to their own husbands in every thing.
> 25. Husbands, love your wives, even as Christ also loved the church, and gave himself for it;
> 26. that he might sanctify and cleanse it with the washing of water by the word,
> 27. that he might present it to himself a glorious church, not having spot, or wrinkle, or any such thing; but that it should be holy and without blemish.

28. So ought men to love their wives as their own bodies. He that loveth his wife loveth himself.
29. For no man ever yet hated his own flesh; but nourisheth and cherisheth it, even as the Lord the church:
30. for we are members of his body, of his flesh, and of his bones.
31. For this cause shall a man leave his father and mother, and shall be joined unto his wife, and they two shall be one flesh.
32. This is a great mystery: but I speak concerning Christ and the church.
33. Nevertheless let every one of you in particular so love his wife even as himself; and the wife see that she reverence her husband.

It is clear from this passage that Christ's relationship to his church has everything to do with the relationship of a husband and wife in marriage. Let's examine Christ's relationship to his church.

We learn that Christ, as the husband of his church, is her head. His wife, the church, is therefore subject to Christ and is called to submit to him. This relationship is not hard to understand and, to those who are in Christ by faith, is not objectionable either. It is a sweet relationship.

By means of his death and resurrection, Christ earned the right to be head over all things to the church (Eph. 1:20–23). Christ sits exalted in the heavens at God's right hand and rules over all with the might and authority of God himself. But Christ's headship over the church is unique. Christ rules over the heathen with a rod of iron to break them in pieces as a potter's vessel (Ps. 2:9). Christ's headship over the church is that of grace. He rules over his church in his great love for her. He protects his bride, cares for her, and communes with her. He dwells with her, carefully leads her, and gives of himself to her. In fact, in his love for his bride, Christ laid down his life for her.

Although the love of Christ characterizes his headship, nevertheless to Christ belongs the authority and right to make decisions for his bride, the church. He rules. Christ says to his bride in John 14:14, "If ye love me, keep my commandments." Christ as head, therefore, determines the spiritual direction in which he leads his church. He bears the responsibility before God, whose will he performs, to lead and direct his church to the end when he will come again on the clouds of glory to receive her into heaven.

Nor does the church chafe under this headship of Christ. Her calling in her marriage to Christ is to submit to his rule. She does so gladly. The Spirit of Christ dwells in the hearts of God's saints, and when Christ says, "Keep my commandments" (John 14:15), they follow their Lord with joy. The fellowship they share together with their husband is close and intimate.

Believers do not view the rule of Christ as a burden. They do not speak out with loud and argumentative voice against him, questioning whether the way he leads them by the word of God is best. They subject themselves to the rule of Christ by submitting to God's word with a meek and quiet spirit.

Oh, it is true that *unbelievers* in the church may speak out against the rule of Scripture over them. They will attempt to follow others than their Lord. They will rationalize why they do not have to obey Christ in certain instances. Israel did this repeatedly in the Old Testament. But believers who have come to taste and see the gracious rule of Christ over them bow humbly before their husband and follow him.

The earthly relationship that a husband and wife share in marriage flows out of their relationship with Christ in the covenant. Christ and his church are one flesh with each other. Together they *live* as one flesh in that covenant relationship: Christ as head and his church as subservient to his headship. What a beautiful and harmonious relationship! Who would question God's wisdom in this relationship? Those who share in such intimate union with Christ bask in it! We would not want it any other way!

Christ intends to give us a taste of this blessed relationship when he joins together in one flesh a husband and his wife. God's command to married couples is this: "Let every one of you in particular so love his wife even as himself; and the wife see that she reverence her husband"

(Eph. 5:33). Only in this way will the relationship of a husband and wife reflect the marriage of Christ and his church.

This means that every husband and wife must view this instruction of Scripture as their *calling* in marriage. When they enter into the marriage bond, foremost upon their hearts must be the calling that they willingly must fulfill toward one another throughout their married life. Husbands must love their wives, and wives must reverence their husbands. Each must make every effort to fulfill their calling.

What is the calling of a husband toward his wife in marriage? Very simply: *love* your wife! As much as Christ loves his church, love your wife! "Wait a minute," one might say, "my calling is to exercise the rule over my wife. I am her head. That means I must give orders that must be obeyed." It is true: the husband is the head in the marriage relationship. But your *calling* as the head in marriage is this: "Love your wives, even as Christ also loved the church, and gave himself for it.... So ought men to love their wives as their own bodies. He that loveth his wife loveth himself. For no man ever yet hated his own flesh; but nourisheth and cherisheth it, even as the Lord the church" (Eph. 5:25–29).

This calling of a husband toward his wife cannot be emphasized enough. Since the fall, man by nature is a tyrant. According to his sinful flesh, he rules with severity and harshness. A tyrant exercises authority with rigorousness, sometimes with ferocity and oppression. This is specifically why the command comes to husbands: *love* your wives!

There is never an excuse for a husband to tyrannize his wife! Never! Today more than ever our society is filled with spousal abuse. This sin also creeps into the confines of the church. A husband may not oppress his wife in any way. That husband who strikes his wife in anger commits a heinous sin. The husband who bullies his wife, uses harsh and hurtful language, humiliates her in front of others (or even in private) crushes her soul. Such a husband will be judged by God in his anger. This behavior toward a wife, in every case, is unacceptable.

Exercising headship certainly implies the authority to rule over a wife. First Corinthians 11:3 says: "But I would have you know, that the head of every man is Christ; and the head of the woman is the man; and the head of Christ is God." But that rule is properly exercised in the way of gentleness, kindness, understanding, and humility. This is the way Christ exercises his headship over his bride the church.

The reason for this is clear: the wife is the weaker vessel. She is easily broken. Peter writes: "Likewise, ye husbands, dwell with them according to knowledge, giving honor unto the wife, as unto the weaker vessel, and as being heirs together of the grace of life; that your prayers be not hindered" (1 Pet 3:7). This verse demands that husbands give honor to their wives. Not only is a wife called to honor her husband, but the husband is to give honor to his wife, too.

Peter gives two reasons. First, she is the weaker vessel. She is a most precious but fragile vase. Physical brutality is only one way a husband can terrorize his wife. He can also dash his wife in pieces emotionally, psychologically, and spiritually. She is the weaker vessel. But the second reason is important too: she is an heir together with her husband of the grace of life. She is precious in the sight of Christ! As far as salvation is concerned, she is her husband's equal. For these reasons a husband must be understanding and gentle with his wife in every way in his relationship with her.

This creation of the woman teaches *the husband* the reason God gave him his wife. She was created a help meet for him. This implies headship, of course. The woman was created for the man and not the man for the woman. But that the woman is a help to her husband does not mean she is his personal slave. Rather, the woman was created to be of assistance to her husband. It was not good that man was alone. He lacked. He needed someone in his life to assist him, to fill the void in his life. God brings to a man his wife because she is perfectly adapted to fill in where he lacked, to be strong when he is weak, to hold him in check when he is apt to stray, to give him wise counsel in his decisions. Men ought to hold their wives in high esteem for the place of honor God has given them in marriage.

When a husband treats his wife in this way, it opens the way for his wife to fulfill her calling to submit to him. When a husband leads his wife in love and understanding, she joyfully submits. Not that her calling depends on this, but how much more pleasant for the wife when a man dwells with her as a man of understanding.

That submission is the calling of a wife toward her husband is clear from Scripture. "Wives, submit yourselves unto your own husbands, as unto the Lord" (Eph. 5:22). "Therefore as the church is subject unto Christ, so let the wives be to their own husbands in everything" (Eph. 5:24). "Let...the wife see that she reverence her husband" (Eph. 5:33). "Likewise, ye wives, be in subjection to your own husbands" (1 Pet. 3:1).

This relationship of the wife to her husband is ridiculed, scorned, and ignored in our present society. Feminism has made deep inroads into the world and the church. Its godless teaching is that the wife is not only an equal in marriage, but that she is the real head. The media portrays husbands as empty-headed, bungling idiots who know nothing of home or children while wives take control in a level-headed manner, saving the day where the husbands utterly fail. Either that or husbands are unfaithful, evil, conniving men whose behavior always threatens the marriage and from whom the wife must flee with her children.

Indeed, just as fallen man apart from Christ is a tyrant, so also fallen woman apart from Christ is a rebel. This sin is found in her sinful flesh. This is why Eve, immediately after the fall, was reminded by God in Genesis 3:16, "thy desire shall be to thy husband, and he shall rule over thee." God-fearing wives who have tasted of the blessed relationship of God's covenant with them must delight in the place God has given them in marriage. The Form for the Confirmation of Marriage used among Reformed churches explains how a wife is to behave toward her husband in marriage:

> In like manner must you who are the bride know how you are to carry yourself towards your husband, according to the word of God. You are to love your lawful husband, to honor and fear him, as also to be obedient unto him in all lawful things as to

> your Lord, as the body is obedient to the head, and the church to Christ. You shall not exercise dominion over your husband, but be silent, for Adam was first created and then Eve, to be a help to Adam.... You shall not resist this ordinance of God, but be obedient to the word of God.[1]

Believers today might read this injunction of the marriage form with tainted eyes. Because we are too often conditioned by the present culture in which we live, we may look at this instruction as belonging to a bygone era when men were male chauvinists. But the instruction quoted here out of this form is "according to the Word of God." God's word is neither culturally conditioned nor time-sensitive. A wife is called to love her husband by showing him honor and respect as head in the relationship. She may not dominate him but must humbly submit to his will. Peter teaches us that a woman adorned with a meek and quiet spirit is in the sight of God of great price (1 Pet. 3:4). A man that finds this kind of virtuous woman has found a ruby!

When a wife complains, argues, and does her work in the home begrudgingly, it places a tremendous strain on the marriage relationship that can often end in anger and bitterness. Solomon's proverb holds true: "It is better to dwell in the corner of the housetop, than with a brawling woman and in a wide house" (Prov. 25:24). A husband must love his wife tenderly, giving honor to her as the weaker vessel. His heart safely trusts in her (Prov. 31:11). The wife is called to love her husband by doing him good and not evil all the days of her life (Prov. 31:12). In this way she honors him as her head.

When husband and wife dwell in the covenant of marriage in their respective callings, they will find a joy in marriage that gives them an earthly taste of the blessed relationship that God's people share with Christ.

---

1 Form for the Confirmation of Marriage, in *The Confessions and the Church Order of the Protestant Reformed Churches* (Grandville, MI: Protestant Reformed Churches in America, 2005), 307.

Is Scripture out of touch with reality when it teaches us this? Is this a romanticized picture of marriage that is found only in fairy tales? Many will say so. They will contend that there is no marriage that is able to reach that ideal! Men and women are sinners. Marriage is always going to be fraught with bitter arguments and quarreling. A peaceful marriage is impossible. Really? Those who speak in this way have not discovered why God instituted marriage: "that each faithfully assist the other in all things that belong to this life and a better."[2] There is no greater joy and intimacy that can be found in an earthly relationship than marriage!

This does not mean, of course, that marriage is not work. God has united together into one flesh two sinners who, by nature, have it in them to clash. Sometimes conflict arises in marriage as a result of sin. When this happens, a man and woman who fear God may not forget their callings in marriage: the husband must deal with his wife as a man of understanding, and a wife is to submit to the will of her husband. *That resolves conflict*! It is not all that complicated—unless we wish to make it so. When we forget our callings, bitterness and strife build up more and more in marriage.

There are four virtues that husbands and wives must exercise in dealing with each other.

The first is giving. Husbands, first of all, are called to give to their wives as Christ gave of himself for his wife, the church. This giving is not just the chivalrous willingness to die for one's wife, however. It is a selfless, daily placing the needs and desires of the wife before his own.

But the act of giving ought to characterize the wife too. She also must give of herself selflessly in order to please her husband. The woman of Proverbs 31 gave of herself not only to her husband, but to her family and even her servants.

As believers we need to be reminded of the need to give in marriage. We live in such a selfish age! Men and women are self-centered

2 Form for the Confirmation of Marriage, in *Confessions and the Church Order*, 306.

and narcissistic. When they enter marriage, it is often with the attitude, "What am I going to get out of it," rather than, "What can I contribute to this relationship to make my spouse happy?" For this reason, marriage is hard work. Those who enter into marriage with the romantic notion that this bond will automatically make them happy soon find out they were sadly mistaken. To make a marriage happy requires giving of yourself.

This means, second, that marriage is sacrifice. When joined into one flesh, a husband is not his own but belongs to his wife. A wife is not her own but belongs to her husband. They both are called to give up the freedom of single life. They do not go their separate ways in marriage. They now walk together as one.

There are certain pursuits I may have enjoyed as a single man or woman, but now I give them up in order to establish my marriage in the Lord. Husbands and wives ought not to be off doing their own thing all the time. Yes, they have the freedom to enjoy life with godly friends, but this freedom ought not to take them away from each other to the extent that they almost live separate lives. Sacrifices must be made in order to be home with each other. The relationship established in marriage is that of friendship. Husbands and wives must be best friends!

The third virtue that ought to characterize us in marriage is faithfulness. This includes sexual faithfulness. Many marriages in the church are threatened by this heinous sin. Society around us is given over to fornication and adultery. Men and women speak of it freely. Movie stars portray it in movies and their personal lives. We can read of it in books and magazines. It is flashed before our eyes in advertisements. Pornography is readily available on the computer or the smartphone. Illicit sex is molding our society in such a fashion that no one can imagine life without it. Even believing husbands and wives can become calloused to it.

In this world of sin, husbands and wives are given the call to faithfulness in their marriage. Husbands may not have wandering eyes. Women ought not to adorn themselves in such a way that they attract the lustful stares of men who are not their husbands. Just as our attention is fixed on Christ in our relationship with him, so also must our attention be fixed on our spouse in the marriage relationship.

Finally, a chief characteristic of a believing husband and wife must be a willingness to forgive. Paul's command to the members of the church applies especially to a husband and wife in a marriage: "Put on therefore, as the elect of God, holy and beloved, bowels of mercies, kindness, humbleness of mind, meekness, longsuffering; forbearing one another, and forgiving one another, if any man have a quarrel against any: even as Christ forgave you, so also do ye" (Col. 3:12–13).

All these virtues must characterize a husband and wife in their relationship with one another, but above all the godly virtue of a willingness to forgive. Husbands and wives in their sin often do not treat each other as they ought. They need to recognize and confess their sins to one another. As their anger begins to cool, they must be quick to admit to one another that they sinned against God and each other. They both must confess their wrong (not just one of them) and be quick to forgive.

"Yes, but it is not that easy! It is more complicated than that! Sometimes my husband or wife has hurt me so badly that it is not so easy to let the matter go!" It is true that bitterness and contempt can result when the sin is great. But true confession of sin reveals itself in humble sorrow, turning from sin, and renewal of life. When such sorrow over sin reveals itself, we are called to forgive. "But I can't!" Yes, you can! "Even as Christ forgave you, so also do ye."

Our callings in marriage must reflect Christ and his relationship with the church in the covenant. How often have we sinned against Jesus Christ! We together with the publican in the temple cry, "God be merciful *to me* a sinner!" We confess with Paul that we are the chief of sinners! "If we confess our sins, he is faithful and just to forgive us our sins, and to cleanse us from all unrighteousness" (1 John 1:9). What an amazing act of grace! We are forgiven, though completely unworthy. God's word to husbands and wives is "So also do ye." Forgiveness must be given in the seemingly minor quarrels of a husband and wife. Forgiveness needs to be sought and given when serious faults have been committed. This is a rule of Scripture that governs married persons. Reconciliation must be the sought-after end in all troubling matters.

It is obvious from all of this that marriage is not a fairy tale institution that automatically brings joy and happiness. Marriage is hard work! Husbands and wives must labor to make their marriage happy. When they work at their relationship, marriage will bring the greatest delight. It will give stability, security, and contentment. No wonder Scripture describes our relationship with God and Christ in the covenant as that of marriage.

—

Chapter 4

Children: God's Heritage

Just as God's covenant has much to say about the intimacy of the marriage relationship, so also it teaches us of a proper and godly parent-child relationship. This is true because in his covenant with us, God is our heavenly Father and we are his dear children. The Bible in many places compares the fellowship God shares with his people in his covenant with that of a father and son.

This is true of God's relationship with his church as a whole. The church is God's son. When instructing Moses to go to Egypt in order to place before Pharaoh Jehovah's demand to let the nation of Israel go, he told Moses to say, "Thus saith the LORD, Israel is my son, even my firstborn: And I say unto thee, Let my son go, that he may serve me: and if thou refuse to let him go, behold, I will slay thy son, even thy firstborn" (Ex. 4:22–23). Now, this was said of Israel, of course, because this nation was seen by God in Christ, who is God's only begotten Son. But it reveals to us just how close a relationship God shares with his church. The church is God's precious son who is the apple of his eye.

This is true of the church as a whole only because it is made up of believers, all of whom are God's children. There is abundant testimony to this truth in Scripture. One of the most beautiful passages that shows this is Romans 8:14–17,

14. For as many as are led by the Spirit of God, they are the sons of God.

15. For ye have not received the spirit of bondage again to fear; but ye have received the Spirit of adoption, whereby we cry, Abba, Father.
16. The Spirit itself beareth witness with our spirit, that we are the children of God:
17. And if children, then heirs; heirs of God, and joint-heirs with Christ; if so be that we suffer with him, that we may be also glorified together.

Many other passages can be added to this. This is also why Jesus teaches us to address God triune as "Our *Father* who art in heaven."

This bond we share with God is a blood relationship. Nothing describes this better than Exodus 24:8, "And Moses took the blood, and sprinkled it on the people, and said, Behold, the blood of the covenant, which the LORD hath made with you concerning all these words." God's people are covered in the blood of the Lamb. The blood of Christ has reconciled us to God. We who were enemies of God are covered in the blood of Christ and now have become God's very own children. "But now in Christ Jesus ye who sometimes were far off are made nigh by the blood of Christ" (Eph. 2:13).

It is true that Christ alone is the natural Son of God, but we through his blood have also become the children of God—through adoption. Through the work of justification, Christ removes the guilt that alienated us from God. Through this same work, God imputes to us Christ's righteousness, making us worthy recipients of his great love and care. Add to this the truth that in union with Christ we have become flesh of his flesh and bone of his bone. In a real sense, we have miraculously and mysteriously, through Christ's blood, become the very children of God!

In this relationship of God's covenant, God is the Father. He rules over his household and children. That God is head in this relationship is a truism. He is God, after all! To him belongs all honor and glory in his family in heaven and on earth.

Children: God's Heritage

As Father, God cherishes his children. There is no deeper love a parent can have for his children than God has for us! He has loved us from eternity with an eternal love. Nothing will ever separate us from that love. He loved us so much that he poured out his eternal wrath on his only begotten Son—the Son of his love—in order to reconcile us to himself.

We are the "apple of his eye." This phrase is used several times in Scripture to describe God's people. The apple of a person's eye is the pupil of the eye, that part through which we observe the world around us. For that reason, our eyesight is precious to us. We love, cherish, and protect it. We are quick to guard our eyes from anything that may ruin our eyesight. God's people are the apple of his eye. They are most precious to him! For that reason, God cherishes them as his precious possession.

Our Father God is also quick to protect his children. He will not suffer their enemies to triumph over them. As he was with Pharaoh, God is indignant with all those who would seek to hurt his children. The Psalmist sings of this care of God in Psalm 121:7–8, "The LORD shall preserve thee from all evil: he shall preserve thy soul. The LORD shall preserve thy going out and thy coming in from this time forth, and even for evermore." For that reason, God will never suffer our feet to be moved. He that keeps us never slumbers or sleeps. His watchful eye is always on us, protecting us from harm.

Out of this love of God for his children flows his pity. God always deals with his children in pity. For some reason, the term "pity" carries with it a bad connotation in our society today. This is expressed in the sharp retort, "Do not pity me!" or "I do not want your pity!" This implies that the one showing pity does so in a condescending way, as if his status is a step above mine and therefore I am an object of charity.

This idea of pity, however, is far from the true definition of this term. Pity is feeling for others in their needs. It is expressed in words and actions of care and compassion. True pity is not condescending but exudes understanding and mercy.

This pity God reveals toward his children. Psalm 103:13 says, "Like as a father pitieth his children, so the LORD pitieth them that fear him." Our heavenly Father knows us well. He knows we are frail and our days are like the grass. He knows that there is sin in us and that we often stumble in our ways. But "the LORD is merciful and gracious, slow to anger and plenteous in mercy. He will not chide: neither will he keep his anger forever. He has not dealt with us after our sins; nor rewarded us according to our iniquities" (Ps. 103:8–10). God dwells with his children as a Father of compassion and understanding.

In that same love for us, our heavenly Father guides us in our way. He gives us his word and commandments. He equips us with the Spirit of truth in order that we might walk in the right paths. At times, in our foolishness, we disobey God and think that our own way is right. Then, as we will find, God chastens and restores. He does so because, as our Father, he directs us in the ways of righteousness.

At times also, we believe our heavenly Father's ways are hard and unyielding. They can cause pain and sorrow, and we do not always understand how they are for our good. But then, by God's grace, we know that God is our Father who loves us and we rest in this truth: "Nevertheless I am continually with thee: thou hast holden me by my right hand. Thou shalt guide me with thy counsel, and afterward receive me to glory" (Ps. 73:23–24). Somehow, some way, God works all things together for our good and our salvation.

As our heavenly Father, God nurtures us as his children. He cares for our needs, supplying us with all that is necessary for life in this world. He provides us with food, shelter, and clothing. Jesus instructs us that we need not worry about what we should eat or drink or with what we should be clothed. Our heavenly Father knows we have need of these things and provides us with them just as he does for all the creatures of his hands (Matt. 6:25–34).

God also provides us with what is necessary for the life to come. He pours out upon us all the blessings of salvation. God provides for and sustains us physically and spiritually. But God also trains us in the ways that lead to life everlasting. He does not leave us on our own to find our own way. He saves us, giving us the spiritual ability to discern the differences between right and wrong. He gives his word to his children in order that they might know the good and acceptable will of God for them. In this way, our Father teaches us the way we should go.

There is one more way that our Father deals with the children of his covenant in his great love for us: he disciplines us! Hebrews 12:5–8 says,

> 5. And ye have forgotten the exhortation which speaketh unto you as unto children, My son, despise not thou the chastening of the Lord, nor faint when thou art rebuked of him:
> 6. for whom the Lord loveth he chasteneth, and scourgeth every son whom he receiveth.
> 7. If ye endure chastening, God dealeth with you as with sons; for what son is he whom the father chasteneth not?
> 8. But if ye be without chastisement, whereof all are partakers, then are ye bastards, and not sons.

God's discipline of his covenant children comes to us in various ways. At times, God mildly exhorts us, reminding us of our calling as his children. Think of Romans 12:1, "I beseech you therefore, brethren, by the mercies of God, that ye present your bodies a living sacrifice, holy, acceptable unto God, which is your reasonable service." Sometimes he sharply rebukes his children, as in James 4:4, "Ye adulterers and adulteresses, know ye not that the friendship of the world is enmity with God? whosoever therefore will be a friend of the world is the enemy of God."

Other times there is a need for harsher discipline. God administers suffering and affliction, not necessarily, mind you, because he is punishing us for one particular sin—although sometimes our sin can bring down upon us immediate temporal chastisement. God sends us suffering in order that we might be reminded of our need to rely upon him for all things. He chastens us sorely in order to preserve us holy unto himself.

Such is how God deals with us as our Father.

In this relationship of God's covenant, we who are the children of God also have our place. We love our Father with all our hearts. We trust him completely and unconditionally. Though his will for us at times does hurt, nevertheless we know that all things will work together for our good because we trust the good and wise ways of our Father. We know that God will do us good all the days of our lives. We have no fear but expect that God will protect us from our enemies. When the world or our sin seems so overwhelming, we flee under the shadow of God's wings and trust him. From the ends of the earth we can cry unto him, knowing fully well that he will lead us to the rock that is Christ for comfort, strength, refuge, and safety. That is why we love our God. He has worked this love in our hearts!

For that reason, we as his children give honor to our Father too. We stand in awe before our God and respect him. With reverence we bow before him and expect all things from him. There is no god like unto our God! As believers we are proud to call him our Father. When he speaks to us, we fear him. Yes, there is a bit of trepidation when he speaks. He is God, after all! But we know he loves us, and the fear we possess is one of childlike reverence.

In reverence, therefore, we also obey him when he commands us. He is our Father and we are his children. We seek to please him by walking in the way of his commandments. Yes, we know that, because of all our many failures, God is pleased with us only for Christ's sake. We certainly do not serve God perfectly as we ought. But Christ through his Spirit does work in us a desire to walk in a way that pleases our heavenly Father.

This is why we bow silently under God's chastening. We know the tendency of our sinful flesh to stray into ways of sin and disobedience. When God chastens us, we humbly submit. We understand our need for it: "Now no chastening for the present seemeth to be joyous, but grievous: nevertheless afterward it yieldeth the peaceable fruit of righteousness unto them which are exercised thereby" (Heb. 12:11).

We will deal with the sufferings we are called to experience in life in another chapter.

It is already clear to us how all of this translates into the parent-child relationship we are to establish with our homes. God is our example in this aspect of our life within the covenant and church too. As parents and children in the home, we are called to imitate the example of our heavenly Father.

Do you love your eyesight? Is it precious to you? Do you carefully protect your eyes from harm? So ought we to love the children God gives us as parents of his covenant. They must be the apple of our eye!

Yet the wicked world boasts of its love for children too. "Everything must be done for our children," it is said. Our society builds hospitals strictly for the care of children. Children who suffer childhood diseases are heralded as "superheroes." An entire secular psychology is developed around proper child rearing.

But, despite all this, who can ignore the horrible abuse of children in this world? In reaction to increasing domestic violence, governments pass laws and develop social services to deal with abused children and the heinous crimes committed against them by angry, violent parents (who insist that they love their children). Parents neglect their little children by sending them to a daycare so that the parents may pursue their own goals and desires in life. To protect children from neglect and abuse, the State has taken ownership of our children in order to protect their rights. School teachers, nurses, and doctors are recruited by the State as unofficial agents to help search out abuse. In an instant, children can be removed from the home by the State, never to return home again if Social Services does not deem it necessary. All of this, once again, because of the horrendous condition of those families who claim to love their children but seriously neglect or abuse them.

Some of these sins can be found in the church of Jesus Christ too, sad to say. Not every parent who sits in the pew on Sunday with his children in their fine Sunday apparel is a believer. What may look exemplary to others outside of the home is different from the reality found within the home and family. There can be child abuse within the realm of the church institute too, most often by hypocrites in the church, but also by fathers and/or mothers who fall into the sins of the wicked. What terrible shame such parents bring upon themselves and the church! But it can happen.

Setting this aside, however, believing parents who consciously live in covenant fellowship with God as their Father love their children as God loves them. Yes, they love their children because there is a natural blood-bond between them and their children. The Bible refers to this as "natural affection" (e.g., Rom. 1:31). Children are flesh of their parent's flesh and bone of their bone. A natural bond of love exists beyond that of the brute beast, since man is a thinking, willing creature. It is a bond that endures. Even when children are grown and married, the blood ties between parent and child are never completely severed. So strong are these ties that believing parents in their weakness will sometimes even wrongly support their wayward children in their sin.

But the love of *believing* parents for their children goes far beyond mere natural affection. Their love is rooted in their life in God's covenant. The Psalmist refers to this in Psalm 127:3, "Lo, children are an heritage of the LORD: and the fruit of the womb is his reward." Because God chooses his people in the line of continued generations in the church, believing parents view their children as *God's* children. They are God's inheritance to them. They are a precious gift of God to them.

God gives children to godly parents in order that they might nurture them in the fear of his name and for his service in this world. Parents who present their infant children for baptism promise to see their children brought up in the doctrines of the Scriptures, as taught in their church, to the *utmost of their power* because they view their children as children of God's covenant. They are given the solemn calling to bring forth the next generation of Christ's church. This is why Solomon continues in Psalm 127:5, "Happy is the man that hath his quiver full of them: they shall not be ashamed, but they shall speak with the enemies in the gate." A man and his wife find joy in their children. Nothing in this world—not money, houses, or fame—is more precious to a godly man and his wife than their children.

This will bear directly on the way such parents bring up their children in their homes. They will utilize their time and efforts to nurture their children as those who will stand as God's representatives in the next generation. They will go to great pains to sacrifice themselves and their own pursuits for the sake of their children—a willing and joyful sacrifice. They will protect their children from the spiritual foes that surround them, teaching their hands to war as spiritual soldiers of Christ. The home will become a training ground for children of God's covenant.

Everything we say and do as parents will shape the lives of our children. God forbid that we mishandle our children by molding their impressionable minds to follow after the wicked world in its ways! We must carefully nurture them in the ways of God and his word. This takes conscious, sanctified effort.

First of all, we are called as parents to instruct our children. This instruction is given in both a formal and informal way. Parents must take time to teach their children the word of God. Much of this instruction is given while they are little and under the direct tutelage of mother and father. Songs of Zion must be sung, teaching their little hearts the praises of God. Bible stories can be told or read to them. Time must be spent reading the Bible to them.

Nor does this formal instruction end when our children reach school age. Parents may not relinquish their calling to instruct their children to the Christian school as if their responsibility has now ended and it is in the hands of teachers to continue that education. Sound Christian schools greatly assist in this task, but they do not replace instruction in the home.

Likewise, the church and its catechetical instruction does not take the place of the duty of parents to be active in the formal instruction of their children. God says of Abraham in Genesis 18:19, "For I know him, that he will command his children and his household after him, and they shall keep the way of the LORD, to do justice and judgment; that the LORD may bring upon Abraham that which he hath spoken of him." Of parents the Psalmist writes in Psalm 78:4–7,

> 4. We will not hide them from their children, shewing to the generation to come the praises of the LORD, and his strength, and his wonderful works that he hath done.
> 5. For he established a testimony in Jacob, and appointed a law in Israel, which he commanded our fathers, that they should make them known to their children:
> 6. that the generation to come might know them, even the children which should be born; who should arise and declare them to their children:
> 7. that they might set their hope in God, and not forget the works of God, but keep his commandments.

Formal instruction in the word of God by parents is a necessity in the nurture of children of the covenant.

Second, parents properly nurture their children by means of their godly example. How true is the axiom "actions speak louder than words." If a father is surly and mean to his family, his sons will grow up to be the same and probably even worse. If a mother screams and complains, her daughters will imitate her when they become wives and mothers. If parents enjoy the lust-filled music and the filth of Hollywood on their television, no amount of instruction in holiness and chastity will teach their children to be godly.

Example is everything! Children are natural imitators. A man and his wife may appear pious to everyone around them, but what goes on in the confines of the home and family will not escape the attention of children. On the other hand, when a man and his wife live a life of piety in the home, this example too will be followed by their children. Such piety, of course, must be tempered by wisdom. For example, when a child walks in disobedience, a parent can speak piously to that child about what the Bible teaches about obedience and feel that is enough, when in reality that child needs to be disciplined for his or her rebellion.

That leads us into the third way parents of the covenant nurture their children: the way of discipline. What does our heavenly Father teach us as parents to do with our children when they disobey him? When our children disobey God's commandments and word, they are not simply disobeying us but they are disobeying God. How must we deal with rebellion in our children?

There are different forms of discipline that ought to be utilized by parents. These forms must correspond with the nature of the wrong that is committed. Sometimes a rebuke is necessary—a mild scolding. Other times, a sharp admonition is needed. Such an admonition often is supplemented with a "milder" form of discipline, such as being sent to their room for a while. Wisdom is needed in discipline. Harsh discipline is not always the answer to every wrong that a child may commit.

When a child, however, is rebellious toward parents then he must know that he is rebelling against God. This may require a "spanking" or "paddling." Solomon in his wisdom gives us this instruction. In Proverbs 22:15, he says, "Foolishness is bound in the heart of a child; but the rod of correction shall drive it far from him." Nor is this simply Solomon's good advice. It is God's inspired word to parents in the case of a disobedient child. Listen again: "The rod and reproof give wisdom: but a child left to himself bringeth his mother to shame" (Prov. 29:15).

Such discipline is far from abuse. It is administered, first of all, out of love for the child and a spiritual concern for his soul. It is administered for the purpose of correction and not out of uncontrolled anger. It is not administered to hurt or wound the child, but in order to chasten him. When applied properly to the backside, it will not result in broken arms or ribs, nor will it result in open welts where it is applied. When a parent applies such chastening properly, it will yield the peaceable fruit of righteousness in their children.

One thing more needs to be said about the way that parents deal with their children. God teaches us in his own treatment of us that we are to pity our children. We must deal with them in an understanding and merciful way. We must be mindful of their human frailty and their faults. Our admonitions and discipline may not be overly harsh, so that as a result our children are afraid of us. When our children are hurting, they should freely come to us for refuge and strength to find sympathy and comfort. When a child is constantly criticized, he or she will quickly withdraw into themselves, lacking confidence and worth. Parents need to be supportive, patient, and attentive to the needs of their children, just as God our Father is to us.

Believing parents do not need to use the secular books and magazines of today's unbelieving world to learn how to raise children properly. The unbelieving sociologists teach an altogether different way of raising children than what the Scriptures teach. The word of God gives wisdom and discretion in all the various ways we are to nurture our children in the fear of God. With our salvation, the Spirit of Christ gives us wisdom to be able to apply the principles of Scripture in a godly way in our homes. Likewise, the older mothers and fathers of the church, who, from firsthand experience, have gained wisdom in this whole area, can teach the younger parents of the church much better than the professionals of this world (Titus 1:3–5). When was the last time you went to your parents or grandparents to ask advice in raising children?

In the sphere of covenant life, parents are also precious to their children. Children and youth in whom God has worked by his grace understand that parents are not enemies when they constantly warn us from ways of sin. Children of the covenant who share a life of friendship with God do not detach themselves from parents and give them passing obedience while losing themselves in their own trivial pursuits. The fifth commandment is to honor father and mother. This is right in the sight of our heavenly Father who gives us this command. "Children, obey your parents in the Lord: for this is right. Honor thy father and mother; (which is the first commandment with promise) that it may be well with thee, and thou mayest live long on the earth" (Eph. 6:1–3).

Out of a deep reverence for the mother and father God gives us, we willingly receive their instruction. We bow humbly beneath their discipline. We give thanks and praise, both to them and to God, for the role they play in our lives. When we observe the shattered lives of children in homes outside of the sphere of the covenant, we ought to be quick in our prayers to thank our heavenly Father for godly parents who are genuinely concerned with our spiritual welfare. Especially as young people, we are reminded that we must always hold our parents in the highest esteem. This is the relationship of fellowship we must share with parents.

Chapter 5

The Blessing of Home and Family

The communal life shared by family members in a believing home is also rooted in their enjoyment of God's covenant with them. For that reason, Satan levels his fiercest attacks against this life within the home. He knows that if he can destroy the life of love and fellowship carried on by families within the confines of their homes, God's covenant with children and children's children will be lost.

These attacks of Satan upon the home are showing themselves successful in the church today. Covenantal life is quickly disappearing in many families of the church. No doubt much of this is due to the influence of the world upon our families. The sins of the world have moved from the theater to the living room to our pockets.

At the same time, some of the blame for this is also due to forgetfulness of the old ways. "I remember when life was much simpler and centered in the family," the old saints say. The young simply chuckle at such references to a bygone era and rush on in the myriad of activities that have now replaced life in the home. The warning of Scripture ought to be heeded: "Thus saith the LORD, Stand ye in the ways, and see, and ask for the old paths, where is the good way, and walk therein, and ye shall find rest for your souls" (Jer. 6:16).

The old paths are those of God's covenant with his people. Throughout the history of the church, God has always lived or dwelt with his children. Adam and Eve in Paradise shared without sin the fellowship of God's covenant (Hos. 6:7).[1] Enoch walked with God. Noah walked with God in an evil age. God established his covenant with Abraham. In the nation of Israel, the tabernacle resided in the middle of the camp, three tribes encamped on each side of it. In this concrete way, God revealed to his people that he lived and dwelt among them. Later, in Canaan, the temple was built in Jerusalem at the very heart of the kingdom. We well know that the glory of God dwelt in the Holy of Holies in the house of God.

God lived and dwelt among his people then—so much so that David could write in Psalm 84:10, "For a day in thy courts is better than a thousand. I had rather be a doorkeeper in the house of my God, than to dwell in the tents of wickedness." Or again in Psalm 27:4, "One thing have I desired of the LORD, that will I seek after; that I may dwell in the house of the LORD all the days of my life, to behold the beauty of the LORD, and to enquire in his temple." Why was this true of David? Because in the house of God he could experience his Father's lovingkindness and favor. He could fellowship with God there.

Is it any different today? When Christ was sent forth by God to dwell among us, he came as our Immanuel. He was *God with us.* God came in the person of his Son and walked among men! We can but imagine the joy of the disciples who believed that Jesus Christ was the promised Messiah and the Son of God. They saw the glory of God and communed with him in the Person of his Son!

I know we might say, "But that was then. We live now. How does God dwell with us now?" In an even more intimate way than when Christ walked among men. Christ informs his church in John 16:7, "Nevertheless I tell you the truth; it is expedient for you that I go away: for if I go not away, the Comforter will not come unto you; but

---

1 The KJV translates Hosea 6:7 in this way: "But they like men have transgressed the covenant: there have they dealt treacherously against me." In reality, the term "man" in this verse is correctly translated "Adam." It would read then, "But they like Adam have transgressed the covenant." This indicates that Adam shared in God's covenant with him.

if I depart, I will send him unto you." The Comforter is the Spirit of Christ whom Christ sends forth into the heart of his church and into the heart of every believer! By means of that Spirit, Christ does not walk by our side but dwells *in us*! God dwells in his church. He dwells in the hearts of his people. In that way, God shares his covenant life with his children.

Scripture defines this relationship of God's covenant as that of friendship. God is a friend of his children in Christ. Yes, he is our Father and we are his children. Yes, this demands of us respect, honor, and obeisance. But God is also a friend to his children. God explains to Israel in Isaiah 41:8, "But thou, Israel, art my servant, Jacob whom I have chosen, the seed of Abraham my friend."

As a friend to his children, God communicates with them. He is present at all times sharing his life, love, thoughts, and concerns with his children by communicating with them. He does not simply take a moment here and there to speak a word to his children. Communication is not merely speaking to someone. To communicate is to transmit thoughts to others in such a way that they understand them and, in turn, reciprocate with their thoughts. To communicate is to convey one's feelings toward others in such a way that they experience them and, in turn, respond with similar feelings. This is the relationship of friendship God shares with his children.

David writes: "The secret of the LORD is with them that fear him; and he will shew them his covenant" (Ps. 25:14). Repeatedly God tells us his children that he will never forsake us in our need. God communicates that to us! In Isaiah 41:10, he says: "Fear thou not; for I am with thee: be not dismayed; for I am thy God: I will strengthen thee; yea, I will help thee; yea, I will uphold thee with the right hand of my righteousness." In his word, God rebukes us in his love. He encourages us. He instructs us. He constantly expresses his deep love and concern for us. In addition, by his Spirit God speaks within us in a way we understand and experience, assuring us of his love. Paul says in Romans 8:16–17, "The Spirit itself beareth witness with our spirit, that we are the children of God: And if children, then heirs; heirs of God, and joint-heirs with Christ." Even in the deepest woes and sorrows of life, God is present, communicating to us his care and strength.

As a result, we as children respond by crying "Abba, Father" in our needs and cares. We join in the prayer of Psalm 61:1–3, "Hear my cry, O God; attend unto my prayer. From the end of the earth will I cry unto thee, when my heart is overwhelmed: lead me to the rock that is higher than I. For thou hast been a shelter for me, and a strong tower from the enemy." The believer bows silently before God in prayer and speaks personally and with understanding with his heavenly Father. There is a life of love and friendship within the family of God. God's children run to their Father with their joy and victories. They flee to their Father with their hurts and burdens.

In all of this, God shares in our lives! What wonderful blessings are ours as we belong to his household and family. What joy we share with him there!

The man who once has found abode
Within the secret place of God
Shall with almighty God abide,
And in his shadow safely hide.[2]

He enters our rooms at night when we are lonely and places his hand on us, assuring us of his care. He holds us in his bosom and gently rocks us when we weep with hurt and grief, soothing us with words of comfort: "I am here and will turn even this to your profit." God's ear is always open to our cry, and he always responds, in Scripture and by his Spirit, with words we need to hear. Our Father is our friend—the closest and dearest friend we will ever have!

One other truth. God expresses his communion with his children in a concrete, earthly way by eating and drinking (supping) together with them. For example, in order to seal his covenant with the nation

---

2 No. 248:1. In *The Psalter.*

of Israel, God had Moses, Aaron, Nadab, and Abihu with the seventy elders of Israel go up into Mount Sinai and meet God there. We learn in Exodus 24:11 that they ate there in his presence. Again, when the tabernacle was erected, the table of showbread, an important piece of furniture in the holy place, was set in place. Upon the table of showbread was spread a cloth of blue. The dishes, spoons, and bowls were put in their places. Each day the Levites made bread and set the table with twelve loaves, symbolizing the twelve tribes of Israel. This symbolized to the nation of Israel that God supped with them in his house, keeping *communion* with them.

During the last passover supper, Christ broke bread and poured out wine as a sacrament to be celebrated by the church of Jesus Christ throughout the New Testament. Each time the church gathers around the table of the Lord to eat and drink, we do so *in communion* with our heavenly Father through the broken body and shed blood of our Savior. We sup with our heavenly Father. Jesus pointed out to his disciples at that last passover meal that the Lord's supper is but a foretaste of the feast we will eat together with our Father when the church is gathered in at the end of time (Luke 22:15–16). God's blessed fellowship with us is experienced in a real and earthly way when we gather about the Lord's table. God has chosen to dwell with us, and we with him, by means of the body and blood of Jesus Christ.

God's friendship with his children in his family becomes more than a mere model we follow. It motivates us to establish homes of the covenant where this same life is enjoyed between members of the family. Often money is spent to build elaborate houses with the latest of amenities: showers with Bluetooth music and heated floors, kitchens with spacious granite counter space, bedrooms with large walk-in closets. But we can have the latest in comforts and luxuries while the house remains merely a house, a large empty space that people cohabit in. Little is done in the kitchen because the family goes out to eat or orders in almost every night. Living space is utilized for watching television or playing on one's devices. At the end of the day, everyone at different hours crashes in their beds, only to get up and rush off to school, sports, or too long a day of work. The result is that the house never becomes a home, in the true sense of the word, where families live and interact with each other. Everyone cohabits but communication seldom takes place. This is *not* a reflection of God's life of communion and fellowship with his children.

Personally, I muse on the "old paths" (since I was born into those times). My mother was busy in the kitchen preparing meals for the family. She cleaned the house. She took time out to play with or read to her children. She had the songs of Zion on her lips. When we came in from a day of playing outside, we could find her there, busy with her tasks as a wife and mother in the home. My father would come home at the end of a day of work, change his clothes, and work on various things in the house and yard that needed fixing. Yes, my mom wore her apron. She was always dressed neatly. "No woman in the office is going to outdo me!" she would say. My mother would teach us our catechism and my father would examine us to ensure that we knew it before we went to class.

The point is, there was love and fellowship shared in the home and family. Was it perfect? Not at all! But it was there. I realize that the world reflects back on those times, giving a hearty laugh at how backward and unenlightened society was then. Many in the younger generations of the church join in its laughter when they compare it with their homes and families now. But here is the question we ought to ask: what best reflects the life of God within his family? Is the modern concept of life within the family better than the life that once was shared in the home and family? Think of Jeremiah 6:16 again: "Thus saith the LORD, Stand ye in the ways, and see, and ask for the old paths, where is the good way, and walk therein, and ye shall find rest for your souls."

Parents must establish the proper atmosphere in the home by spending time with each other and with their children in the confines of their house (home). No one may or can replace the presence of mother and father together in the home with their family. It is true that there are extenuating circumstances that may keep father late at work at times. There may be illness or death that disrupts the family unit and life in the home. In these circumstances, God gives grace to carry on. But that must not be the norm. Time and effort must be exerted to make the home a place of safety and security. It must be a sanctuary to which our children can flee in order to escape the peer pressure and the temptations of the wicked world outside of the home, a place where everyone can simply be themselves.

With this, parents must establish the proper *spiritual* atmosphere in the life of their family in the home. In connection with our too-busy lifestyles, emphasis is given to individual devotions. It is said that we must take time out in our individual lives to read the Bible and pray. And this is true! This is a must. Personal devotions are necessary. But it seems very little emphasis is placed on *family* devotions anymore—fathers taking time to lead their families in the reading and study of God's word and in prayer. This too is a *must* in a believing family, since by doing so we take time together to fellowship with the God who fellowships with us.

Some years ago, I had a conversation with a young woman of the church who had recently broken off a dating relationship with a young man of the church. In the course of our conversation, she explained to me why she put a stop to the relationship. Though this young man came from a home that was to all appearances exemplary in its church attendance and life in the church, nevertheless they never spent time in the home praying. The young woman asked her boyfriend if he would pray before each date and he defiantly replied, "I don't know how to pray! We never pray in our home!" When she asked him if his family had devotions together, he answered, "Once in a while, during our Sunday afternoon meal, if we have the time."

This is why I specifically brought up the fact that in Scripture God often reveals his fellowship with his people while eating and drinking with them. It's true that having family devotions around the table at the conclusion of our meal is a tradition. We may utilize any time of the day to gather with family to read God's word and pray together. But time *must* be taken each day to do this. The recommended time to do this is when we are gathered around the table with food and drink and commune with each other and with our God. Is this not what the psalmist prescribes in Psalm 128:3–4? "Thy wife shall be as a fruitful vine by the sides of thine house: *thy children like olive plants round about thy table.* Behold, that thus shall the man be blessed that feareth the LORD."

Family dinner is not only a time when we can read and discuss God's word as a family, but also an important time to raise before God petitions concerning the family and church. What family does not have difficulties at times with one another or with others in the church? We have friends, fellow saints, and relatives who suffer afflictions by God's hand and others who mourn. Family devotions give us time to pray together in order to bring before God our needs and cares. A believing home must share in covenant fellowship with God—and with one another. Sitting around the table provides an excellent opportunity to laugh, discuss, and even argue together as a family. How important this is for life within the family!

In all of this, parents need to establish the bond of friendship with their children, just as God is a friend. Jesus Christ is our friend "that sticketh closer than a brother" (Prov. 18:24). This does not mean, of course, that parents ought to be buddies with their children by acting like kids themselves. Our children are called to respect their parents, just as we in God's family must bow before him with reverence. But this does not mean that parents cannot be friends of their children. On the contrary, they must establish the relationship of friendship with their children.

This cannot be accomplished when there is no communication and fellowship within the home. The millennial generation has also become known as the therapeutic generation—a generation seeking advice from therapists. The need for therapists, counselors, and psychiatrists indicates a deficiency in the families of our world. Dysfunctional families lead to a dysfunctional society that seeks out "professionals" to do the work that parents ought to do in the home. In a believing home where proper relationships are established, there is nothing more therapeutic than children talking with mom and dad. Mothers and fathers of God's covenant must make time to listen to their children and give them the advice needed in the various circumstances of life. This kind of communication requires a healthy spiritual relationship between husbands and wives, parents and children, and siblings in the home. If this is no longer true in the home, what has become of the blessed truth of God's covenant as it must manifest itself in the families of believers?

Conversations in the home must have spiritual substance! Sure, some discussions will be lighthearted. It should be that way in a godly home. Other discussion, however, must be of a serious nature, addressing spiritual concerns. This does not begin when children are in their teens. It is too late for parents to try to discuss something with their adolescent children if they never spent any serious time with their children when they were young. Parents must talk with (not at) their children already when they are little. They must maintain open communication with them in all the various stages of their lives. They must see to it that they are *friends* to their children—closer than any other friendship their children have with their peers. Remember, God is a friend to his children! Parents must imitate our heavenly Father to whom we can flee as his children with every hurt and care. Parents must labor diligently with their children in order that when the time comes that they are hurting or confused, or even when they have sinned, they will seek them for wise counsel and even forgiveness.

Parents must never give their children the impression that they are too busy, thus forcing their children to seek advice from someone else. The peers of our children, even if they are godly, are not equipped to give the wise counsel that believing parents, who have experienced the pressures and concerns of life, are able to give.

Together in the home, children are taught by godly example. They are taught to pray. They are taught spiritual values. They are taught to live in harmony with others in the home and church. No doubt this requires of parents self-sacrifice and conscientious labor. They must especially sacrifice their time to be with their children. But even as Christ has sacrificed himself for us to be closer than a brother, so also parents must be willing to sacrifice themselves to make their family a place of blessed fellowship—a place that reflects God's friendship and fellowship with them.

When we live in the consciousness of God's covenant with us, our families will have a unique appearance. Our homes may not mimic the world. A family that truly shares together in fellowship with each other will experience in a real way what it means to share in God's love and friendship. What counselor or therapist can impart that joy to a person? By way of a covenant home and family, God also chooses to continue his covenant in the line of our generations.

—

Chapter 6

Tempered by Adversity

Adversity is a part of life in this sin-cursed world. It not only falls upon the wicked who live apart from God, but it also strikes the homes and families of God's people in this life. Another word used several places in Scripture is "affliction." These terms identify everything that causes anguish, pain, and suffering. As a result of adversity or affliction, our souls become disquieted and cast down. Some afflictions affect our bodies as well, but even these can cause grief and sorrow of heart. Sometimes the hurt of adversity is so deep that we are overwhelmed. Like the Psalmist, we cry out to God: "Deep calleth unto deep at the noise of thy waterspouts: all thy waves and billows are gone over me" (Ps. 42:7). Our souls can be cast down and disquieted in us (Ps. 42:5).

God sends adversity upon individuals and families in diverse ways. We surely cannot begin to enumerate all the hardships, small and great, God sends upon us. Our pathway through this life is narrow and characterized by sharp and unexpected turns. Sometimes the way is rocky, difficult, and long. At times affliction is short. At other times it can last a lifetime. There is one thing that is certain: no one can escape adversity.

There are countless physical afflictions people bear: birth defects, accidents that leave a person handicapped, diseases of all kinds—some debilitating, others that slowly take our lives. Hebrews 11:35–38 lists persecutions God's children can bear:

35. Women received their dead raised to life again: and others were tortured, not accepting deliverance; that they might obtain a better resurrection:
36. and others had trial of cruel mockings and scourgings, yea, moreover of bonds and imprisonment:
37. they were stoned, they were sawn asunder, were tempted, were slain with the sword: they wandered about in sheepskins and goatskins; being destitute, afflicted, tormented;
38. (of whom the world was not worthy:) they wandered in deserts, and in mountains, and in dens and caves of the earth.

Persecution is one of the cruelest afflictions a person is called to bear.

But then there is also the affliction of soul. This affliction bombards us from every angle: financial problems, troubles in our relationships with others in the workplace, church, school or worse, in the home. When friends turn on us and forsake us, when children forsake the Lord and rebel, when spouses abandon or abuse us, when the church, once faithful, embraces error—all these and many more cause us anguish of heart and soul. This pain and grief of the heart can lead some to deepest depression—a dark place that few can understand.

Then there is death. For the believer, the door of death is but a brief moment from this life into the next. Christ has overcome the power of death for us. But in the wake of the death of a loved one there is grief, sorrow, and loneliness for those left behind. The earthly bonds have been severed, and we are called to carry on in this world without our loved one. Life on this side of the grave is, as the Heidelberg Catechism in Lord's Day 9 so aptly describes it, "a vale of tears."[1]

It is not my intent to explain in depth the purpose of God in affliction, but a brief explanation of this is necessary if we are going to

1 Heidelberg Catechism Q&A 26, in Philip Schaff, ed., *The Creeds of Christendom with a History and Critical Notes*, 6th ed., 3 vols. (New York: Harper and Row, 1931; repr., Grand Rapids, MI: Baker Books, 2007), 3:316.

understand the relationship of God's covenant within a family when he sends us adversity.

First of all, we must understand that adversity of every sort is the result of sin entering into this world. When we reach heaven, the "former things will have passed away," namely, sin and its effects. For that reason, in heaven all tears will be wiped away from our eyes, and there shall be no more death, neither sorrow, nor crying (Rev. 21:4). All of these are true for us now because sin has entered into this world and death by sin.

This means that man is to blame for the afflictions we bear in this life. It is not because of the cruel hand of God. This is the answer we give to that person who, in pride, refuses to bow before his Creator because he feels that a God who allows these terrible things to happen to a person is not worthy of worship. All these hardships in life, the evils present around us, are due to man's disobedience and rebellion against God.

That being said, of course, God as God is in sovereign control of these evils he sends us in this valley of tears. What the wicked man receives from the hand of God he deserves. God uses the good things he sends the wicked as well as the bad to lead him in the slippery ways of destruction.

But why would God send these adversities upon his children? Why must we experience these horrible hardships of life? When we view them properly, we will receive but a glimpse into the gracious workings of God. The adversities the believer experiences in this life, due to the presence of sin in this world, God actually turns to our advantage (see Heidelberg Catechism, Lord's Days 9 and 10).

We learn in 2 Corinthians 4:17 that "our light affliction, which is but for a moment, worketh for us a far more exceeding and eternal weight of glory." God uses our affliction to work, shape, and mold us for our places in eternal glory! We must look at ourselves as rough-cut gems that God shapes through the laser of affliction to be those perfect jewels that make up his crown. This is why the Psalmist could write in

Psalm 119:71, "It is good for me that I have been afflicted; that I might learn thy statutes."

Solomon explains adversity from another point of view in Ecclesiastes 7:13–14, "Consider the work of God: for who can make that straight, which he hath made crooked? In the day of prosperity be joyful, but in the day of adversity consider: God also hath set the one over against the other, to the end that man should find nothing after him." God sets adversity over against prosperity in our lives in order that the joy of prosperity might not draw us away from God to place our hope in the things of this present world.

How true it is that when everything seems to be running smoothly and we indulge in our prosperity, when we hear from our lips, "life is good," we can lose a proper perspective on life. Our dependence on God and our prayers become weak and meaningless. But when God tempers our prosperity with adversity, as he often does, then the prayers of the believer are lifted up to God more fervently and more often! When we suffer cares and burdens of this life, we draw near to God and look to him for our strength.

Affliction is for our profit! The writer to the Hebrews expresses this in terms of our heavenly Father chastening us through affliction in order that it might yield in us the peaceable fruit of righteousness (Heb. 12:5–11). In this way, God actually uses our suffering in this present life to work for us the glory that awaits us in heaven.

More can be written on the purpose of God in sending adversity in the life of his people, but our intent here is to direct our attention to how we, as the children of God's covenant, deal with such affliction when God sends it upon us or a member of our families. What does the covenant teach us when the waves and billows of life overwhelm us?

It is simple really. We hear God say to us: "I am your God. You are my child. I will never leave you; I will never forsake you in your deepest hour of need! If your closest friend forsakes you, or even if father and mother forsake you, I will take you up."

God has spoken these words of promise to his saints repeatedly in their times of need. When it seems impossible to carry on in life, God speaks to us the comforting words of his promise spoken to the troubled saints in Israel: "When thou passest through the waters, I will be with thee; and through the rivers, they shall not overflow thee: when thou walkest through the fire, thou shalt not be burned; neither shall the flame kindle upon thee. For I am the LORD thy God, the Holy One of Israel, thy Savior" (Isa. 43:2–3).

When the believer falls on his knees before God in sorrow and grief over his sins, God assures him by his Spirit, "Go your way, your sins are forgiven you." When fear of his enemies causes distress in his life, God strengthens him. As Moses says in Deuteronomy 31:6, "Be strong and of a good courage, fear not, nor be afraid of them: for the LORD thy God, he it is that doth go with thee; he will not fail thee, nor forsake thee." When tribulation, distress, disease, terminal illness, poverty, or such like befall the child of God, God responds to his need quickly. He flies on the wings of the wind and sends from above and draws him out of many waters because Jehovah is his stay (Ps. 18). Nothing shall separate us from the love of God that is in Christ Jesus (Rom. 8:39).

Some who read this know experientially the pain that can rack our bodies. Some know of the inner hurt and sorrow that builds up in our souls due to our own sin and the sins of others. Who can begin to describe the inner hurt of those who have been abused in marriage or as children? Others know of suffering when they are called to face death.

It is not an easy matter for us to sit by helplessly and watch a loved one slowly taken from us due to cancer. The loss of one taken suddenly by a heart attack or an accident—sometimes when they are little children, sometimes in youth, sometimes when they are a young father or mother busy with a family—is heart wrenching! Such loss wrings from our hearts overwhelming pain that knots the stomach, makes the chest ache, and brings floods of tears to our eyes. How can we go on with life? For weeks it seems impossible to carry on with the normal activities of life. The loneliness of a widow or widower or of a single saint in old age is an emptiness that others cannot always appreciate.

What then is the comfort that can overcome all this? Where does the believer find strength to carry on? In the truth of God's covenant with him or her. God dwells with us. He shares his favor, love, and fellowship with us always—especially in times of weariness and distress.

But more. Believers live in this world of toil and sorrow with hope! Hope is waiting and longing for something we have not yet received or do not yet experience. That hope is also found in God's covenant with us. It is the hope of eternal life. Before the heart of God's people is the realization that heaven is the place where God brings his covenant with his people to its perfect end or goal.

God's people are pilgrims in this world, only passing through to the place we long and wait for in heaven. In heaven there will be no more suffering of adversity. It will be a place of perfect fellowship with God—a place of eternal peace and rest. The afflictions of this present life actually serve, then, to remind us that we have no abiding place here. Our home is heaven. That is the place of our longing.

In hope the believer flees to God in affliction with this request: "Hear my cry, O God; attend unto my prayer. From the end of the earth will I cry unto thee, when my heart is overwhelmed: lead me to the rock that is higher than I" (Ps. 61:1–2).

This is the sure response of the believer to hardships in life. We are not like those who refuse to be comforted in this life when troubles surround us. We do not respond to these troubles in a sinful way. We do not seek our own way out of these difficulties. We do not turn to the world to find the answers. These will only bring us to more misery.

We cry unto the Lord. We commune with him on our beds when our eyes are held awaking. Again the Psalmist speaks. We read in Psalm 4:4, "Stand in awe, and sin not: commune with your own heart upon your bed, and be still." The result? Psalm 4:8, "I will both lay me down in peace, and sleep: for thou, LORD, only makest me dwell in safety."

How does a family deal with adversity? Through prayer and meditation on God's word, we run beneath the shadow of God's wings. In faith, we cling to the assurance given us in God's word. We are his children chosen in Christ, saved from wrath. We are covered in the blood of our Savior. All things are for us because God is for us.

We confront affliction, therefore, first of all, with quiet brave endurance, committing our ways unto the Lord. All suffering works patience, James teaches us. Now, we must let patience have her perfect work in us. Webster defines patience in its various facets: "Bearing trials calmly and without complaint; manifesting forbearance under provocation; not hasty or impetuous; steadfast despite opposition, difficulty or adversity." All of these descriptions apply to the reaction of the believer to adversity in its every form, even when it is caused by the sin of another. Why patient in adversity? Because we are held in the everlasting arms of God! He will not suffer our feet to be moved. He will be our guide even unto death. Without that knowledge, our afflictions will only lead to complaining—and even to resentment with God's ways with us. This ultimately leads to straying from God and his commandments.

A second way we deal with adversity in life is by contentment. Scripture extols this virtue in the life of a believer when confronted with troubles. It is worth reminding ourselves of the various afflictions the apostle Paul bore in his life for the sake of the gospel. These are listed for us in 2 Corinthians 11:23–28,

> 23. In labors more abundant, in stripes above measure, in prisons more frequent, in deaths oft.
> 24. Of the Jews five times received I forty stripes save one.
> 25. Thrice was I beaten with rods, once was I stoned, thrice I suffered shipwreck, a night and a day I have been in the deep;
> 26. in journeyings often, in perils of waters, in perils of robbers, in perils by mine own countrymen, in perils by the heathen, in perils in the city, in perils in the wilderness, in perils in the sea, in perils among false brethren;
> 27. in weariness and painfulness, in watchings often, in hunger and thirst, in fastings often, in cold and nakedness.

28. Beside those things that are without, that which cometh upon me daily, the care of all the churches.

Very few have had to endure as much adversity as Paul. In the face of all of this, Paul could write in in Philippians 4:11–13,

11. Not that I speak in respect of want: for I have learned, in whatsoever state I am, therewith to be content.
12 I know both how to be abased, and I know how to abound: everywhere and in all things I am instructed both to be full and to be hungry, both to abound and to suffer need.
13. I can do all things through Christ which strengtheneth me.

Contentment is resting in the Lord, humbly walking in the path he has chosen for me without rebelling. It is trusting that God is good and wise in the way that he leads me. After God had taken everything away from Job, his reaction was: "The Lord gives, the Lord takes away. Blessed be the name of the Lord."

What a different reaction that is compared to the selfish unbeliever of our world today, who is quick to blame everything that goes wrong on someone else. "I fell from a ladder and broke my leg. I'm going to sue the company for producing such a rickety ladder!" Far-fetched? Not in our world today! It is always someone else's fault that I suffer. How quick the wicked are to complain and even rave about others when something causes a wrinkle in their lives.

In contrast to this, the believer learns that godliness with contentment is great gain (1 Tim. 6:6)! We are God's people, the sheep of his pasture. His ways may not be known to us. They may be in the sea (Ps. 77:19). But God leads us, his sheep, even using the suffering of this present time to keep us safe within his fold. All things are for our sakes who belong to Jesus Christ. This ought to work in our hearts peace in the ways God leads us, even when those ways are adverse.

The third way the child of God deals with adversity in life is that of wisdom. Wisdom is that virtue of using the knowledge we possess in a prudent way to produce good results. When God sends affliction in our lives, we use the knowledge of God's covenant, that is, his care for and fellowship with us, to cast our cares upon him and make decisions concerning our suffering that are in accordance with his will.

Here are examples of foolishness. "My job offers very little in the way of pay. I cannot cover the bills. I am going to take the little that I have to the casino and try to make lots of money quick"—a violation of the eighth commandment. Or again: "I am no longer happy with my spouse. He or she ignores or neglects me. I can no longer live under this duress so I will divorce him or her and go out and find another"—a violation of the seventh commandment.

That is not how a believer deals with suffering in life! When adversity strikes, the child of God uses God's word and the knowledge that everything is under his sovereign control to make decisions that are wise, decisions that are according to God's word. When we bow under the heavy hand of God, he uses adversity to our profit and will turn it to our advantage.

Is it easy to suffer? Not at all! No chastening for the present is joyous, but grievous. Hebrews 12:12–13 says, "Wherefore lift up the hands which hang down, and the feeble knees; *And make straight paths for your feet,* lest that which is lame be turned out of the way; but let it rather be healed."

There are many aspects to what we have now written as far as life in the family is concerned. We certainly have not covered all of these in detail. There are many books—some good, many bad—written on the subject of the family. Secular books on the subject can be discarded immediately. They deny the wisdom that is from above. Even many Christian books do not use Scripture as their basis but instead are filled simply with the advice of men or women. In this section of this book, I have attempted as much as possible to ground the Christian family in the word of God, not only but specifically from the viewpoint of God's covenant. It is my prayer that those who in their lives "taste and see that God is good" as they live within the blessed covenant of God established with them and their children will come to a deeper appreciation of how God's covenant ought to influence them in their homes. May our families be a reflection of God and his family as he dwells with us in his great love and care.

- Section Two -

God's Covenant and the Church

—

Chapter 7

The Church: The Body of Christ

The doctrine of the church is one of the most ignored and therefore misunderstood truths of the Bible. Even many who maintain the five points of Calvinism care very little about the doctrine of the church.

The result is that many in our day believe they can live without the church. Others are "half-churched." Belonging to a church means nothing more than attending a particular church semi-regularly. They have no obligation to the church and the church none to them. Switching to another church takes nothing more than leaving one place to go to another. Still others attend a church that ignores completely the biblical ecclesiastical structure of the church. The proper offices in the church, the proper functions of the church, and the proper worship of the church are non-existent.

Along with this attitude, there is no regard for observance of the Lord's day as the day God has set aside to "keep it holy." Sabbath desecration is epidemic even among church-goers. Such a careless attitude toward the Lord's day and church membership has created what we find in the church world of today: a falling away from the church, the truth, and finally God himself. Increasingly, the world is becoming antichristian.

Over against this ignorance stands the blessed truth of God's covenant. God's covenant teaches believers what the church is and their need for commitment to and membership in the church. This is true because God establishes his covenant with his church. God's covenant is the intimate relationship of love, favor, and fellowship into which God has entered with his people in Christ. He will be their God and they will be his people.

We have already discovered the joy and security that relationship provides individual believers and families who live in covenant with God. The truth we explore in this section of our book is that God lives in friendship and fellowship *with his church*. No one outside of Christ's church shares in God's love, favor, and fellowship. Believers enjoy the blessings and promises of God's covenant only as members of Christ's church in this world. For that reason, a believer's life within the covenant is also a life within the church. Let's consider how this is founded on Scripture.

First of all, that God establishes his covenant with those who dwell within the confines of the church is founded on election. Before time began, God chose unto himself a certain number of people to share with him in his covenant. He did not choose a mass of random, unrelated individuals to be his people. On the contrary, God elected *as a whole* a special or particular people to share with him in his covenant. That body of people predestined by God to share in his covenant is his elect church. Peter informs the church: "ye are a chosen generation, a royal priesthood, an holy nation, a peculiar people" (1 Pet. 2:9).

The church is God's, *chosen* to be a distinctive people. What makes the church distinctive is that God has elected his church as a whole *to be his family*. He has elected his church in eternity as a family of sons and daughters in Christ. This is evident from Ephesians 1:4–5: "According as he [God] hath chosen us in him [Christ] before the foundation of the world, ...having *predestinated us unto the adoption of children* by Jesus Christ to himself, according to the good pleasure of his will." God has chosen the members of his church as his very own children—separated from eternity to live together as siblings in the household and family of their heavenly Father in a relationship of love and fellowship. Only the elect have the exclusive right to dwell together with God as their Father!

That God has elected us as his children must impress upon the heart of every believer that he or she may not live apart from others who have also been chosen to share in God's love and fellowship. God's elect belong to a body of people set apart by God, a people dedicated and consecrated to serving God *together* in this world. They are brothers and sisters of the same household. This truth itself ought to motivate every believer to join himself with the church of Christ in this world. Believers must see the need to be a part of God's family.

If this is not enough to convince us to be members of Christ's church—and it should be—there is more. God chose to give this family of his elect as a whole to his Son Jesus Christ. He did so because, already in eternity, God chose his people together as a whole in Christ (1 Pet. 2:4–8; Eph. 1:3–12). Never has the church been viewed by God apart from Christ. Never! Not even in God's counsel or plan for all things.

Christ was fully aware of this during his earthly ministry. In his prayer in John 17:6, Christ explicitly says: "I have manifested thy name unto the men which thou gavest me out of the world: thine they were, and thou gavest them me; and they have kept thy word." Or again, in verses 9 and 10, "I pray for them: I pray not for the world, but for them which thou hast given me; for they are thine. And all mine are thine, and thine are mine; and I am glorified in them." John also gives this commentary on Christ's great love for those whom God had given him out of the world—that is, the elect church—in John 13:1, "Now before the feast of the Passover, when Jesus knew that his hour was come that he should depart out of this world unto the Father, *having loved his own which were in the world, he loved them unto the end.*"

The relationship of fellowship that God's elect church shares with God is rooted, therefore, in Jesus Christ. This is confirmed by the truth that the body of God's elect is synonymous with the body of Christ. The church is Christ's body. Ephesians 1:22–23 teaches that Christ is given to be "the head over all things to *the church* which is his body."

That the church is the body of Christ is true by virtue of the fact that every believer is bound together with Christ. God sent his only begotten Son, his natural Son, in order to deliver his elect people out of the horrible bondage of sin into which they had fallen, together with the human race in Adam. Christ performed the work for them on the cross and in his resurrection. By means of this work, Christ earned all the blessings of salvation. Then, at the appointed time in each person's life, Christ sends forth his Spirit to dwell in their hearts. At that very moment, the Spirit imparts to them the blessings of salvation. He regenerates them. He sets them free from the bondage of sin, infusing into them the life of Jesus Christ. At the moment of salvation, the Spirit binds each believer to Jesus Christ. The believer is permanently grafted into Christ, making him one with Christ. Every believer literally becomes one with Christ!

But the body of Christ, just like a human body, is not made up of one member. A body has many members. This is true of Christ's body, the church, too. Paul says in 1 Corinthians 12:12, "For as the body is one, and hath many members, and all the members of that one body, being many, are one body: so also is Christ."

Every person grafted into Christ's body is intimately and inseparably bound together with all the other members of that body of Christ. Think of that. A body is not made up of a finger. A finger can do nothing if it is not attached to the hand. The hand can do nothing if it is not attached to the arm. The arm can do nothing unless it is attached to the body at the shoulder. With our salvation, each of us is grafted into Christ. Christ stands as the head of that body. But the members of God's elect church saved in Christ are members together with others in the body of the church. They cannot function as believers apart from the other members of the church.

What, then, should this truth regarding the church impress upon the heart of every saint? That Christ does not free me from sin to live a life independent of the rest of the body of Jesus Christ. When grafted into Jesus Christ, believers are grafted into his body, the church.

Through our salvation, we are bonded together with others in the church of Jesus Christ. Christ always saves a person *in connection with the rest of the church.*

This does not contradict the personal character of my salvation. What is *my* only comfort in life and death? *I* belong to my faithful Savior. *I* am held in God's almighty hands. *I* need not fear though troubles befall me in this life. Indeed, Christ is my personal Savior. But my salvation is always related to the salvation of the other members of Christ's church. This is why Christ has taught us to pray, "*Our* Father which art in heaven. Give *us* this day *our* daily bread." We recognize our connection with the church.

We can view our place in the church as that of a brick in the wall of a building. As long as we lay there upon the ground, we have no value or beauty. But when the mason places us in the wall of the house and we are seen together with the other bricks, we are valuable. Take any of those bricks out of the wall and there would be a gap. Not alone but together with the other saints, we are beautiful in the sight of God.

A believer does not rejoice in his own salvation, only to live his life apart from the body of Christ, the church, and walk independently of other believers. He recognizes the truth that God has placed him in the church in order that he, together with God's people everywhere, might share in the love and fellowship of God. Together they lift up their praises to God in order that God might glorify himself in his church.

For our benefit when reading Scripture, we keep in mind the various names given to the church of Christ. She is called Zion (Heb. 12:22–23) or Daughter of Zion (Isa. 1:8), God's Son (Ex. 4:22–23), Jerusalem (Rev. 21:2), Israel (Rom. 11:26), the Bride of Christ (Eph. 5:25–27), the Temple of the Lord (Eph. 2:21–22), God's Household or Family (Eph. 2:19), God's Vineyard (1 Cor. 3:5–9), and the list can go on. One cannot read Scripture without being impressed by the truth that the church as a body of saints is a special people gathered from the ends of the earth and called by God's name.

To the elect church (called Israel here), God speaks the words of his covenant in Isaiah 41:8–10,

8. But thou, Israel, art my servant, Jacob whom I have chosen, the seed of Abraham my friend.
9. Thou whom I have taken from the ends of the earth, and called thee from the chief men thereof, and said unto thee, Thou art my servant; I have chosen thee, and not cast thee away.
10. Fear thou not; for I am with thee: be not dismayed; for I am thy God: I will strengthen thee; yea, I will help thee; yea, I will uphold thee with the right hand of my righteousness.

Among the many errors of Arminian thinking is a denial of God's covenant. Most often we do not view the error of Arminianism from this perspective. The Arminian bases his teaching on the premise that God loves everyone and sincerely desires to save everyone. For that reason, God in his grace sent Jesus Christ into this world to die and make salvation available for everyone. Through preaching, God then sincerely offers this salvation to everyone who hears. If a person, through an exercise of his free will, accepts this salvation (said to be an act of faith), then God will save him. One's election depends on whether one accepts Jesus Christ. Election then is conditioned on faith (man's ability to accept Christ). This error in its entirety contradicts the idea that God establishes a relationship of love, favor, and fellowship only with his elect church.

God loves the people of his covenant. He loves the church. God's love is exclusive. He shares his love only with those who belong to Christ. Nor will God reveal his love to the wicked! If he did, what would be the sense of belonging to the church? Christ knew the members of his body, chosen and given him by God. Before going to the cross, he prayed, "Thou hast given him power over all flesh, that he should give eternal life to as many as thou hast given him" (John 17:2).

God loves exclusively those who belong to his elect church. With these alone he speaks the secret of his covenant.

Likewise, the blessing of God's grace is exclusive. In Proverbs 3:33–36 we read: "The curse of the LORD is in the house of the wicked: but he blesseth the habitation of the just. Surely he scorneth the scorners: but he giveth grace unto the lowly." God reveals his favor (grace) only to those whom he has saved in Jesus Christ and to no one else. At the start of his Gospel, John says: "The law was given by Moses, but grace and truth came by Jesus Christ" (John 1:17).

Those saved in Jesus Christ are members of his body the church. God's favor, therefore, is a blessing of God's covenant applied only to those who are members of the church of Jesus Christ. Would God in his favor smile upon those whom he has not chosen as members of his church? Is God pleased with those with whom he has not chosen to share in his covenant? Would God enfold them in his arms and, in his grace, give them any kind of blessing (earthly or spiritual) if they did not belong to him? If God did show his favor toward the wicked in his sin (apart from salvation), what would be the sense of sharing in God's covenant with him? The wicked would then be able to reason: "God loves me, he smiles upon me in his favor, he shares his fellowship with me, even though I am not a member of Christ's church in this world! Life is grand!"

If we have become lost in the details of this chapter, here is a summary of what we have learned:

1. God has chosen, in his eternal plan, a distinct body of people in Christ.
2. God, in his grace, grafts each of his elect people into Jesus Christ by a true faith. As a result, they have become members of Christ's body.
3. This body of Christ is his church, with whom God now shares his covenant.
4. There is no fellowship with God outside of that church. God shares his love and favor with them alone.

What we study in the chapters ahead is rooted in this fundamental knowledge: God's covenant is established with the church as a body of believers. The members of the church share together in the blessings of God's covenant.

—

Chapter 8

The Church: God's Dwelling Place

The Bible uses the figure of a body to describe the intimate relationship of fellowship that exists between Jesus Christ, the head of the body, and believers who are members of his body. This body of Christ is the church. It is made up of God's elect, chosen in Christ and saved in him.

Every believer confesses with the Heidelberg Catechism in Lord's Day 21, I believe "that I am, and forever shall remain, a living member of the same."[1] Out of this confession flows the conviction of every believer, that he is called by God to dwell in the church of Christ as it becomes visible in the church institute. This is true because God's church is also his dwelling place. God and his Son Jesus Christ dwell or live in the church of Christ in this world.

What comforting words of God's covenant God speaks to his church in Psalm 132:13–14, "For the LORD hath chosen Zion; he hath desired it for his habitation. This is my rest for ever: here will I dwell; for I have desired it." The Psalmist here is not speaking directly of the body of God's elect gathered from the nations of this world but refers specifically to the institute of the church as it existed visibly in the nation of Israel. God in his covenant dwells with his people; he is

1 Heidelberg Catechism Q&A 54, in Schaff, *Creeds of Christendom*, 3:325.

their God and they his people *in the sphere of the church institute.* God has desired to inhabit the church as an earthly institute.

As we mentioned in the last chapter, there are many today who no longer are convicted of the need to belong to a church institute or, if they do realize to a degree the importance of such, they are not committed to the church. The church does not become their life. They see no need of the church institute for a life of fellowship with God. They believe that membership in the church requires nothing more than sporadic attendance at the worship services, involvement in a few social programs a church might offer, and having their names placed on a prayer chain. Many *attend* a church but refuse to *join* a church. They have no desire for men (elders) to rule over their spiritual lives. They want the freedom to live as they want, with no requirements laid on them by the church. Belonging to a church institute that requires commitment is not looked on so favorably anymore today.

The Scriptures point out that the elect body of Christ, gathered from the beginning of time to the end, has always taken on institutional form. It did in the Old Testament under the patriarchs and later when the nation of Israel was organized at the foot of Mount Sinai. Christ was born and labored in the church institute, a church ruled over by the elders and chief priests of the people. The church of the New Testament too was instituted immediately after Pentecost, as individual groups of people were organized into congregations or churches (Acts 14:21–23). But what needs emphasis is that through the church institute God chooses to dwell with his people. It is in and through the church institute that God shares his covenant blessing with his people. For that reason, God's people must join themselves to the church in this world.

This is why.

Christ dwells in the church institute in a real, concrete way. It is true that he sits on his throne in heaven. He no longer dwells with his church as he did during his earthly ministry. He rules over her from heaven by his Spirit and word. But Christ as the Head of his church provides for his church in his absence men who can serve his church as his representatives on earth. Christ, therefore institutes—that is, organizes—his church under officebearers. Christ calls and ordains men to serve on his behalf in his church. Christ in a real way *dwells in fellowship with* his church through men called to office in his church. The offices in the church of Christ do not exist by the will of men. Men do not decide the best way to govern the church. The offices of the church are divinely instituted. It is true that there are many different ways that church institutes of today have decided to govern themselves. But there is only one *biblical* way of governing the church. In this way, God chooses to dwell in fellowship with his people in his church here below.

In the Old Testament, the officers of the church were distinctly chosen by means of the ceremony of anointing. A man was ordained to his office by God when oil was poured upon his head by a representative of the church. This anointing signified that he was ordained by God and qualified with the Spirit to serve in his particular office in the church. The first office to which a man was anointed was that of priest. Aaron (Lev. 8:12) and his sons (Num. 3:3) were anointed to their office as priests. This anointing was used subsequently to ordain all the priests into their office. This same anointing was used to call and ordain a king into his office in the Old Testament church. We read of Saul, for example, in 1 Samuel 15:1, "Samuel also said unto Saul, The LORD sent me to anoint thee to be king over his people, over Israel: now therefore hearken thou unto the voice of the words of the LORD." The third office to which a man was anointed in the church of the Old Testament was that of prophet. We read of Elisha being anointed prophet in 1 Kings 19:16.

Through these three offices, God chose to reveal himself in his love and fellowship to the people of his old covenant. By means of the priest's office, atonement was made for the sins of God's people. Believers were reminded that it was only through shed blood that their trespasses were forgiven and they were reconciled to God. They were reminded of God's mercy toward them. It was also by means of the work of the priest's office that God's people had access to God in prayer and therefore could share in God's favor and love.

The kings of Israel ruled over this great nation on behalf of God, exercising justice and judgment, leading them and protecting them against their enemies. No doubt, when the king ruled justly over God's people, they saw God's hand guiding them as a nation and providing for their earthly needs.

The prophets spoke the word of God to his people. Through the mouth of the prophet, God communicated with them and communed with them. They could hear the voice of Jehovah speaking words of comfort and encouragement as well as warning and admonition.

Through each of these offices, God revealed his covenant, his fellowship, his love, and his favor toward his people. God dwelt among them. Psalm 46:5 and 11 say, "God is in the midst of her; she shall not be moved: God shall help her, and that right early.... The LORD of hosts is with us; the God of Jacob is our refuge." Through the offices in the Old Testament church institute, God made the church his habitation.

It is no different in the New Testament.

These offices were fulfilled in Christ, who combined them into his one office of Mediator. He was ordained by God and qualified by the Holy Spirit to be our prophet, priest, and king. Even now, Christ sits in heaven and functions as our Prophet, who by his Spirit and word reveals to us the will of God; as our Priest, who makes continual intercession for us with our Father on the basis of his sacrifice on the cross; and as our King, who governs, defends, and preserves us in our salvation. As a New Testament church, we no longer need men to fill these offices because Christ exercises them over us from heaven.

However, Christ does not leave himself without representation in the church of the New Testament. Christ now replaces the Old Testament offices with new offices, that of pastor, elder, and deacon. Through these special offices in the church, God in Christ chooses to dwell with his people. Christ has chosen to reign over, care for, and speak with his people through these offices.

The elders of the church are under-shepherds of Christ. In faith, God's people look to Christ as the Shepherd and Bishop of their souls. Peter describes the church this way: "For ye were as sheep going astray; but are now returned unto the Shepherd and Bishop of your souls" (1 Pet. 2:25). The work of the elders as Christ's under-shepherds (both pastors and ruling elders) is soul-care. We read in Hebrews 13:17, "Obey them that have the rule over you, and submit yourselves: *for they watch for your souls,* as they that must give account, that they may do it with joy, and not with grief: for that is unprofitable for you."

The spirit of this world is to criticize, ignore, and—worse yet—slander those who serve in positions of authority. At times, this spirit can prevail in the church of Jesus Christ among some of her members. When pastors and elders who faithfully bring God's word are slandered as incompetent and ignorant in their dealings with God's people, incapable of counseling with the word of God, this is an attack on Jesus Christ himself who chooses to administer his care over his sheep through these men. When this spirit of the world begins to prevail in the church, as it did in the nations of Israel and Judah, God is highly displeased with that church and eventually she will fall.

Likewise, Christ has ordained in his New Testament church the office of the pastor and teacher in order that he might communicate with his people. Fellowship always requires communication. When the pastor, each Lord's day, faithfully delivers the word of God, Christ chooses to speak with his people. The word that he brings is a savor of life unto life and of death unto death. It is powerful and accomplishes what God purposes for it to do: to save his people and harden others in their sin. Christ uses the word preached to feed and nourish the humble soul. Christ exercises soul-care through the preaching too.

The prayer of God's people before the worship service begins must always be, "Father, give me a humble heart to *bow beneath* the preaching of the word in order that I might be a hearer of that word. May I not lift up my heart in pride placing myself *above* the preaching as an examiner and judge. Feed me by thy word!" God's saints then listen carefully to the preaching, applying it to their own lives (not to that of the neighbor) in order that they might not only be hearers of the word but also doers. When members feel they have the right to criticize everything the minister says, or how he says it, they are attacking Christ who has chosen to speak through his chosen ambassador.

The deacons are called to administer the mercies of Jesus Christ, lifting up prayers on behalf of God's saints as they care for their earthly and spiritual needs. Those who deny that the office of deacon carries with it the authority of Christ are wrong. This is an *office* in the church. Christ exercises his authority through this office too. Perhaps the authority of the deacon is limited to the support of the pastor and church as well as that of the poor, but when the deacons visit the home of those in need to read God's word and pray with them, they do so with the authority of Christ. Christ exercises his mercy through them. Paul says in 1 Timothy 3:13, "For they that have used the *office* of a deacon well purchase to themselves a good degree, and great boldness in the faith which is in Christ Jesus." The members of Christ's church must see to it that they "lay by them in store as God has prospered them" (1 Cor. 16:2) in order to support the deacons in their labors.

These offices, therefore, ought to be highly honored among the members of the church institute. Without these offices there is no church! It is the calling of every believer to hold the men of these offices in highest esteem and humbly submit to them as they function in these offices. Paul gives this command in 1 Timothy 5:17–20, "Let the elders that rule well be counted worthy of double honor, especially they who labor in the word and doctrine.... Against an elder receive not an accusation, but before two or three witnesses. Them that sin rebuke before all, that others also may fear." Or again in 1 Thessalonians 5:12-13: "And we beseech your, brethren, to know them that labour among you, and are over you in the Lord, and admonish you; And to esteem the very highly in love for their work's sake. And be at peace among yourselves." When members of the church reveal a spirit of rebellion and disrespect toward those who serve in these offices discord, unrest, and division will prevail in the church.

The Bible also teaches that every believer that is joined to Jesus Christ has an office. This office is not instituted by Christ, but belongs to the believer by means of his union with Jesus Christ. Every believer is anointed with Christ's anointing (1 John 2:20, 27), which means that every believer is a prophet, priest, and king in Christ. This is known as the office of believer.

This office places upon every believer two requirements. First, it requires that a believer join himself to the church institute. His office stands in subjection to Christ's office as Mediator. Christ has chosen to exercise his office through the special offices he has ordained in the church institute. A believer therefore subjects himself to Christ's office by joining himself to the church institute. To live deliberately apart from the church institute denies one's own anointing. How can a child of God exercise the office of believer apart from belonging to a church?

Second, God's saints exercise the office of believer within the church institute by exercising themselves in God's word through faithful attendance to the preaching. As prophets, they hear Christ speak to them through his word and then confess Christ's name to others. As priests, having been admonished by the word, they present themselves as living sacrifices of praise to God. As kings, they take God's word with them during the week to fight against sin and Satan.

This means, as we have already explained, that the calling of a member of the church in his office of believer is to submit humbly to the officebearers of the church. The office of believer in his relation to the special offices is not that of an equal. Nor may an individual saint elevate his office of believer over and above the special offices in the church. Yes, every saint has the calling to know God's word. Every believer, when listening in a humble spirit to the word preached in his church and detecting error, has a right to question the pastor and, if need be, the elders concerning the preaching. He has a right to protest and appeal to the broader assemblies of the church. This belongs to him in his office of believer. But this never gives him a right to dishonor or disrespect the offices that Christ himself has placed over him. Every believer is called to honor Christ by honoring those Christ has placed in authority over him in the church. Protest and appeal must be done in meekness and humility. This is the only proper way a believer may behave in exercising his office.

There is one more vital reason a believer must join himself to the church institute in this world: in his great love for his people, God protects and nourishes them within the realm of the church. Christ does this through certain means that he commissions the church *officially* to administer to her members. These are the means of grace. These means belong to God's covenantal care over his people.

The first is the preaching of the gospel. We only mention this means since it is the subject of another chapter. Preaching is the chief means God uses to strengthen, encourage, instruct, and admonish his people in their faith, something so necessary since the activity of faith in us can become very weak due to our sinful flesh. Through the preaching God speaks with his people. As we mentioned, communication is vital to fellowship.

The other means of grace are the sacraments: baptism and the Lord's supper. Both of these focus our attention on God's covenant with his church. Baptism is a sign and seal of the "washing of regeneration" (Titus 3:5). Regeneration is the first work of Christ in our salvation. It is that moment when the Spirit of Christ takes up his dwelling place in our hearts and infuses into us dead sinners the life of Jesus Christ. At that moment, God's elect are cleansed of sin and grafted into the church and covenant of God. The sacrament of baptism signifies that grafting into Christ and God's covenant. Since we are passive in our regeneration, so also is the recipient of the sacrament of baptism. A person is baptized; he does not baptize himself.

Because the sacrament of baptism signifies incorporation into God's covenant, infants of believers are to be baptized. This does not mean the sacrament itself saves infants who are baptized. Nor does it mean to believing parents that God incorporates every baby that receives this sacrament into his covenant and its blessings. It simply is a sign and seal of God's promise to establish his covenant with the children of the church in the line of continued generations.

God regenerates infants (Ps. 22:9–10). "Both redemption from sin and the Holy Ghost, who works faith, are through the blood of Christ promised to them no less than to their parents."[2] Once again, this does not mean that God regenerates every infant born to believing parents. Nor does the sacrament of baptism give some kind of false assurance to parents of the church. This sacrament is a sign and seal of the promise of God that he does save and graft into his covenant children of believers. Believing parents rest on that promise.

The Lord's supper is also a sacrament that focuses our attention on the covenant God establishes with his people in Christ. This is why the Lord's supper can be referred to as "communion" (1 Cor. 10:16–17). The participants enjoy at the table of the Lord communion with God and with one another in the faith. There is a difference, therefore, between this sacrament and that of baptism. Baptism is a sign of the work of God's grace in incorporating us into his covenant. That takes place one time, at the time of our regeneration. We are baptized once therefore. Plus, we are passive recipients of this sacrament just as we are of regeneration. But believers partake of the Lord's supper repeatedly because it is a sign and seal of continued nourishment in God's covenant. In this, believers are active in their faith. They take and eat the bread and drink the wine. This is why only believers who have reached the age of discernment may partake (1 Cor. 11:27–30). This is also why the elders must guard the table of the Lord from those who do not believe, lest the covenant of God be profaned.

We spent some time studying these truths for two reasons. First, in order that we might be reminded that the covenant of God has everything to do with the church institute. The church institute is not some

2 Heidelberg Catechism Q&A 74, in Schaff, *Creeds of Christendom*, 3:331.

man-made organization that has little or nothing to do with our place in God's covenant. Belonging to God's covenant cannot be separated from membership in the church institute.

Second, by examining what the church institute is and what it offers, we pray that we might come to a richer understanding not only of the importance of the church institute for our lives, but also of the beauty of life within the church.

A life of faith in the church institute enriches our life of fellowship with God because it is there that God chooses to dwell with his people. "Beautiful for situation, the joy of the whole earth, is mount Zion!" (Ps. 48:2).

Chapter 9

The Communion of Saints

The church as the elect body of believers and the church visible are not synonymous. Christ's elect church is made up of those exclusively chosen by God from eternity as his own particular people and therefore those in whom Christ has worked faith. The elect body of Christ is made up of true believers only. The church institute is called such because that is where God chooses to gather the elect body of Christ. God chooses to dwell among his people there.

But there is a crucial difference between the church institute and the church as the elect body of believers. The church institute is not made up of believers only. The hard reality is that the church institute also houses unbelievers. Jude 1:4 informs us that in the church institute there are those who "creep in unawares," feigning faith. They are not true believers, though outwardly they may appear as such. Likewise, we realize that others are born into the church that are not believers. Many of these will leave the church ("they went out from us, but they were not of us," 1 John 2:19). But others will stay in the church, living an outward life of conformity to the church and its precepts but not truly finding their life in Jesus Christ. Jesus describes this phenomenon for us in the parable of the wheat and the tares in Matthew 13.

It is for this reason that the gainsayers insist that they do not need to belong to the church institute since it is only filled with hypocrites anyway. This accusation is ungrounded, however. First of all, the church is filled with sinners. Believers within the church institute do not claim to be without sin. They realize that their own sins and inconsistencies can at times be glaring. Believers join themselves to the church institute exactly because they find there other believers who, together with them, cling to Jesus Christ in whom they together find the forgiveness of sins through his cross. They confess their sins, but also confess that they belong to their faithful Savior who has earned for them righteousness and peace with God. When they look for other believers, they find them in the church institute. The accusation that the church institute is filled with hypocrites is also unfounded because the church institute itself does not claim to be free of unbelievers, even though those who truly believe can be found within the church institute.

This does not mean, however, that a believer may join himself with just any church institute. Those who claim that this world is becoming a better place to live because church institutes seem to be growing and exerting more influence on society fail to understand the Scripture's distinction between the true and the false church. Much of Christianity today is apostate. False churches and denominations abound! These churches are filled with teachings and practices that are contrary to the Scriptures.

Just as the kingdom of Israel, and later the kingdom of Judah, turned from serving Jehovah and were destroyed, so also many churches of today are ripe for destruction. In the last days, many false teachers will arise, giving people who have itchy ears to hear something new and exciting exactly what they want. Paul warns Timothy that "the time will come when they will not endure sound doctrine; but after their own lusts shall they heap to themselves teachers, having itching ears; and they shall turn away their ears from the truth, and shall be turned unto fables" (2 Tim. 4:3–4). In such churches that have departed from the ways of God by denying the Scriptures, God no longer establishes his covenant! There is no fellowship with God found there. God's command to believers is to come out from among them.

The discerning believer needs to find a church where God dwells in communion with his people. That church is found only where the pure gospel is preached and maintained, where the sacraments are administered in such a way that God's covenant is placed before the hearts of her members, and where the faithful rule of elders is found. When such a church is found, there also believers are found dwelling together in love. In that faithful church that exhibits these marks is found the communion of saints!

Those who commit themselves to a faithful church find the greatest of delights in that church. They are given by the church institute itself everything necessary for their spiritual lives. That is delightsome! But they also find their life in that church. They live in the church! Not in the same sense that they live within their home and families, of course. But in the sense that their lives center in the church. The church becomes a community of believers. They establish friendships with fellow believers. Their lives center in the activities of the church.

This communion has a highly spiritual side to it. When we confess our faith with the Apostles' Creed, we say: "I believe a holy, catholic church, the communion of saints." The church *is* the communion of saints. It is where saints dwell together in sweet accord. Why is this true? Because we as fellow believers are living within the realm where God has chosen to dwell with us *together.* The church as the body of Christ necessarily implies that this is true of the church institute as well. Believers are members of one another in the body of Christ. Members of the body cannot exist without each other. In fact, they do not wish to exist without each other. When God establishes his covenant, he does so within the church institute as an organism.

An organism has life. The church is not a dead organization that simply carries out certain functions ordered by Christ. There is life in the church—the life of Christ. The organism of the church can be defined very simply as Christ's body of interdependent members, whose relations and life are determined by their function to the whole.

Such is the life that goes on in the church of Christ. Everything that takes place in our individual lives as believers is determined by the function we have together with other members of the church.

Paul describes this in simple terms in 1 Corinthians 12. The ear and the eye need each other. They serve different functions in the body, but they are interdependent on each other for the proper function of the body.

There may be members in the body of Christ that view themselves as less honorable or feeble. Their function in the church, however, is necessary and valuable. If I were to smash my little toe, would not the entire body react to it? That little toe plays its own function in the body, and when it hurts the whole body hurts with it.

That is the organic life that transpires in the church of Jesus Christ. That is how closely related to one another members of the church are in that body! How selfish when one puffs himself up in pride and seeks to lead his life within the body while having nothing to do with that body. That is actually a denial of God's covenant in his own life because he is seeking to separate himself from the life of the church where God establishes his covenant.

Proper conduct in the church, then, flows out of this organic life of the church. Let's explore four different avenues where this holds true.

1. *Spiritual activities.* Bible studies or societies are not official functions of the church. They flow out of the organic life of the church. Believers within the realm of the church desire to meet together and study God's word together. They know that as "iron sharpeneth iron; so a man sharpeneth the countenance of his friend" (Prov. 27:17). Believers therefore seek each other out and join together in a discussion of God's word.

By way of an aside, Bible studies are not a time when the members of the society sit silent and let the leader (minister) give a discourse on God's word. It is a time for lively discussion. Nothing said is too "dumb." It is true that some of God's people do not speak as much. That is perfectly fine. But God's people must come to Bible study ready to discuss with one another the word of God. The leader of the society is there to lead the discussion and then, after some discussion, make sure a correct interpretation of God's word prevails.

The point is that Bible studies are a part of the organic life of the church. The same is true of Sunday school. Catechism classes are an official function of the church and are therefore taught through the offices of the church. Sunday school is taught by qualified members of the church who discuss with our children stories in the Bible. Personally, I think that Sunday school can profitably be used to teach our children, while young, how to discuss God's word, in order that when they reach the age of young people they are ready to discuss that word with each other in society.

There are other functions that flow out of this life of the church. Organizations have been formed within the church to publish periodicals or books. Members of a church might choose to support and/or assist in the structuring and running of an orphanage. One of the most important labors that becomes an integral part of the organic life of the church is the organization of Christian schools. This means, of course, that Christian schools are not parochial in nature, that is, schools that are an official function of the church in her offices. Christian schools are parental. Schools flow out the organic life of believers as they live within the sphere of the church. So important is this aspect of the communal life in the church that we will devote an entire chapter to it.

Inasmuch as these various functions flow out of the life of the church, they are covenantal in character. They are labors that are an integral part of the communion of the saints.

2. *The use of time and talents for the benefit of the church.* God has given to each member of the church certain gifts. Everyone has his or her own set of talents. Those who view themselves as of no use to the church deny the fact that God has set them in the body of the church for the benefit of the church—not themselves, but the church. In our self-absorbed society, the attitude far too often is, "What is in it for me? What am I going to get out of marriage? What will the government do for me? What do I get out of the church?" Believers who belong to

the communion of God's covenant, and therefore the communion of saints, do not join themselves to the church with such a selfish attitude. They are ready cheerfully to use their gifts and talents for the benefit of the church as a whole and for other believers in the church.

Some are given the talents of being able to teach, others to rule. Some men and women are organizers and are good with finances. Some are good with their technological skills. Others are given the ability to work with their hands. Some are writers. Added to this list are spiritual gifts that stand out. Some excel in kindness and gentleness. They are quick to empathize with an individual. Others are given steadfastness. Some have a logical mind, others good old common sense. And the list can go on. Some are given more than one, perhaps even multiple of these gifts. Others may have fewer.

Paul emphasizes in 1 Corinthians 12:4–6 what every believer must keep in mind with regard to the talents God has given him or her: "Now there are diversities of gifts, but the same Spirit. And there are differences of administrations, but the same Lord. And there are diversities of operations, but it is the same God which worketh all in all."

God gives to each of us as believers the various gifts we possess. He requires that we use them on behalf of the church or fellow believers. No, this does not mean free handouts or discounts when it comes to business deals. But it does mean that when I see a brother or sister in need, I help them out, using my talents as much as possible. Besides, the church needs men with special gifts to serve in office. Men must be willing to do this when that need arises.

All of these are obligations that God places upon us as members of the church as we live together in the communion of saints. All of these flow out of the life of the covenant God has established with his church and her members. We help each other and the church readily and cheerfully because we belong to the family of God in this world! We dwell with fellow believers who are our brothers and sisters in the Lord. They are our friends with whom we fellowship—a fellowship that is inseparable from our fellowship with God. God's covenant ought to inspire us to use our gifts and our time for the benefit of the church of Jesus Christ.

3. *Friendships within the church.* If fellow believers are found within the church, it only follows that we must make friends of God's people. The friendship of God's covenant with his people is found in the church. The members of the church share in that friendship *together.* The friendships we seek therefore are with those who also are friends of God.

We will have an opportunity to take another close look at this when we consider what God's covenant has to say about our lives in the world. But Paul asks the question of the believers in Corinth: "What part has he that believeth with an infidel [unbeliever]?" (1 Cor. 6:15). Light and darkness do not mix. All of God's people have been placed by God *in* the world, yet we are called not to be *of* the world.

We all meet plenty of unbelievers as we walk through this life. Everyone wants companionship. Unbelievers at work want to go places with others in the workplace. Unbelieving neighbors want their block parties. Others establish fraternities or unions to join in a common brotherhood of men. But God's people within the realm of the church are given a place to seek out friendships. This is why the young Psalmist writes in Psalm 119:63, "I am a companion of all them that fear thee, and of them that keep thy precepts." Living in covenant communion with God influences the communion I have with fellow saints.

4. *Endeavoring to keep the unity.* When a body is healthy and strong, the members of the body function in harmony with each other. At times, God in his providence lays a person low with a disability called multiple sclerosis, which, among other things, interrupts the communication between the brain and the body. The result is a dysfunctional body. The members of the body do not communicate with each other properly. There is no harmony between them. A person can be severely crippled by this disease.

It is no different in the body of Christ as she becomes manifest in this world in the church institute. The church institute is filled with sinners—redeemed sinners, but sinners nonetheless. Though Christ the head of the body sends forth commands to his members to walk in love and holiness with each other, at times sin acts as a disease that causes members of the body to ignore the mind of Christ that is in them. When this happens, the peace and harmony necessary to function as a church is disrupted, and the church becomes distorted and dysfunctional. That is a sad day for the church of Christ.

Various causes can lead to this spiritual disease in the church. One of the most common is the area of Christian liberty. The church of Christ has been set free from the slavery of the Levitical laws that governed the church before Christ. Today we are no longer under the tutor of the law. This freedom is called Christian liberty.

It is not that we are without law. We must daily apply the law of the ten commandments to our lives. We walk in them to show our love for God and the neighbor. Within the bounds of these commandments (and the various Scriptural admonitions that flow out of them), Christ allows believers in his body today the freedom to wisely apply the various principles of God's word in a way that is best for them. These ways differ from one individual or family to the next. At times, members of the church are quick to judge other members in the way they carry out their life of liberty. Others will stretch their liberty to satisfy their flesh. The result is friction, disagreement, and disharmony between members of the church.

Another cause of more serious concern is doctrinal disagreement in the church. The church of Jesus Christ and her members are clearly exhorted by Scripture that they "should earnestly contend for the faith which was once delivered unto the saints" (Jude 1:3). The church of Christ must always stand upon the truth of Scripture if it is to remain faithful to her Lord. At times in the church, there are those who teach error, some deliberately and others in ignorance. Either way, error must be stopped through the proper forms of discipline. Unchecked controversy in the church causes strife and creates a huge rift between members of the church—so much so that the church is crippled by it. This too is a threat to the unity and peace of the church.

The calling of the church and her members always—no matter what the circumstance—is "to endeavor to keep the unity of the Spirit in the bond of peace" (Eph. 4:3). The covenant God establishes with his people in Christ is a covenant of peace. As he says in Ezekiel 37:26, "Moreover I will make a covenant of peace with them; it shall be an everlasting covenant with them." The church of Jesus Christ is called always to peace and unity.

In the area of Christian liberty, the word of God sets forth the prescription for unity and peace. One such passage is Galatians 5:13–16,

> 13. For, brethren, ye have been called unto liberty; only use not liberty for an occasion to the flesh, but by love serve one another.
> 14. For all the law is fulfilled in one word, even in this; Thou shalt love thy neighbor as thyself.
> 15. But if ye bite and devour one another, take heed that ye be not consumed one of another.
> 16. This I say then, Walk in the Spirit, and ye shall not fulfil the lust of the flesh.

Believers, in love, must allow others their liberty even if they would not walk in the way others do. This they must do *without judging another*! On the other hand, believers do not wish to cause offense to other saints either. They are careful in what they do in their liberty so as not to offend another for whom Christ died.

But what about in the midst of controversy? Does controversy in the church allow brother to rise up against brother in hatred? Do strong doctrinal differences give members of the church the right to *slander* those who oppose them? Does controversy in the church give believers the right to sin by speaking venomous words of anger, bitterness, and strife? Does it give them the right to form factions or parties in the church as happened in the church of Corinth?

Absolutely not! Even in controversy we are dealing with fellow members in the body of Christ for whom Christ has died. The truth must always prevail in the church. But that truth ought to be spoken in love (Eph. 4:15), never in bitterness and hatred. The apostle John was vehement in his defense of this truth. But he also says, "If a man say, I love God, and hateth his brother, he is a liar: for he that loveth not his brother whom he hath seen, how can he love God whom he hath not seen? And this commandment have we from him, that he who loveth God love his brother also" (1 John 4:20–21).

As long as believers are members together in the church of Christ, they must deal with each other as such even in controversy. Why? Because the God of all peace expects this of those with whom he dwells in the church of Christ. Notice the apostle John's doxology in 2 John 1:3, "Grace be with you, mercy, and peace, from God the Father, and from the Lord Jesus Christ, the Son of the Father, *in truth and love.*"

The church of Jesus Christ must love and strive to keep the unity of the church at all costs. A church whose members are always bickering and disagreeing with each other, a church that is always filled with strife and contention, is distorted and ugly! Who from the outside would ever be attracted to such a church? Who among the children of that church would ever want to remain in her?

Christ's bride in this world is beautiful because she is characterized by the holiness and love of Jesus Christ himself. Let this mind be in you that was in Jesus Christ. "Let nothing be done through strife or vainglory, but in lowliness of mind let each esteem other better than themselves" (Phil. 2:3). Every member needs to pray for the peace and unity of the church institute where he or she belongs. "Pray for the peace of Jerusalem: they shall prosper that love thee" (Ps. 122:6).

The communion of the saints is a fellowship we share together within the covenant God has established with his church. What blessed peace and unity prevail when brothers in the Lord make it their delight to dwell there in blest accord, using their gifts for the benefit of others in the body of Christ.

Chapter 10

Frequenting God's House

Of major concern today is attendance at the worship services of the church. At times in history, regular attendance in the house of God waned. In our modern world and society, however, the neglect of worship has reached epidemic stages.

Many will keep their names on the membership role of churches while seldom darkening the doors of the church. Much of this is due to a lack of interest in the things of God's kingdom. There is no longer any desire for the sincere milk of God's word. Church is a bore—especially if it involves a man "rambling" on for a long period of time about some Scripture passage.

Some of this complaint is legitimate, since in many churches men give water for milk in their "preaching." Why go to church to hear a man tell jokes, give moral homilies, and offer human advice? We can find these elsewhere. But whether it be the fault of the preacher or of the members, attendance in church is sorely lacking.

Others give as an excuse the claim that the law of the ten commandments has been fulfilled by Jesus Christ and therefore the fourth commandment to sanctify the sabbath day is no longer in effect for the New Testament church. With the abolition of this law, the necessity of attending the worship of the church also falls by the wayside. If a person chooses to attend church, that's fine, but he or she does not have to do this on any consistent basis. The first day of the week may be treated like any other day of the week. The worship of the church is optional and not a requirement.

Those who have tasted the blessed fellowship of God's covenant do not view worship in this way. Meeting together with God's saints in the house of God is the chief desire of a believer. There truly is no better place on earth to spend his time than in Father's presence, sharing in his love and friendship.

Is that an exaggeration? Not when we look at our worship on the Lord's day from the perspective of God's covenant! The worship of the church is covenantal in nature. The Psalms are filled with this idea. We are the children of God's family who, when we worship, enter into our Father's house to meet with him there. We sing in Psalm 84:1–2, "How amiable are thy tabernacles, O Lord of hosts! My soul longeth, yea, even fainteth for the courts of the Lord: my heart and my flesh crieth out for the living God." And in Psalm 122:1, "I was glad when they said unto me, Let us go into the house of the Lord."

It is true that the house of God in the Old Testament referred to the temple. But Jesus explained to the Samaritan woman at Jacob's well that the time would come when God's people would no longer worship God in the temple in Jerusalem. They would instead worship the Father in spirit and in truth, "for the Father seeketh such to worship him" (John 4:23). This refers to the New Testament church who, when they gather in God's house today, do so in spirit and in truth, worshiping their Father. The idea, however, is the same today as it was with the saints of old: we gather in the house of God in order to meet with our Father there. This is an expression of fellowship with God.

Nor is such worship optional. We may not attend the worship of God's house whenever we feel like it. Worship is a requirement that includes tremendous spiritual benefits for every believer. This requirement to gather in God's house is based, first of all, upon our salvation.

Why does God save a people unto himself? The whole human race has plunged itself into sin. Does God decide to save a few people out of the human race in order to make them happy and leave the rest behind in their misery? Is that why God saves? Is it not rather that God does everything in order to glorify his name in the earth?

From eternity, God chose a people in Christ that would share in his covenant with him. God saves them as a people unto himself in order that, through them, his name might be glorified in all the earth. That is God's purpose in saving his people, that through them he might bring glory to his name. How? By means of their praises! We learn of that in 1 Peter 2:9, "Ye are a chosen generation, a royal priesthood, an holy nation, a peculiar people; *that ye should shew forth the praises of him who hath called you out of darkness into his marvelous light.*" This is why God calls his church from the ends of the earth! When the church of Jesus Christ gathers in worship on the Lord's day, the praises of God ring forth throughout the earth. Through those praises, God glorifies himself in all the earth.

But there is another reason God saves us. He saves his people in order to share in his most blessed fellowship with them. There is no better place on earth to be found than where God's children sit beneath the feet of their Father in his house, worshiping him together! As a result of their salvation, believers crave to be in church worshiping God.

At the time of this writing, a COVID–19 virus rages in the world, and God's people are forced to refrain from public worship at this time. The hearts of God's people ache that they are restrained from entering into God's courts of praise. We understand in a small way what the Psalmist was experiencing when in exile in Babylon, far from the house of God:

1. By the rivers of Babylon, there we sat down, yea, we wept, when we remembered Zion.
2, We hanged our harps upon the willows in the midst thereof.
3. For there they that carried us away captive required of us a song; and they that wasted us required of us mirth, saying, Sing us one of the songs of Zion.
4. How shall we sing the Lord's song in a strange land?

5. If I forget thee, O Jerusalem, let my right hand forget her cunning.
6. If I do not remember thee, let my tongue cleave to the roof of my mouth; if I prefer not Jerusalem above my chief joy. (Ps. 137:1–6)

True believers *love* to be in God's house! They are glad when they hear the call to prayer. They say to themselves, let us go up to God's own house and bow before him there (Ps. 122).

So much is it the desire of the believer to enter into fellowship with God that when they are called by the church to worship, they do not balk at the opportunity to do so. Often I am asked why the churches of which I am a part call our members to worship two times each Lord's day. My answer is simple: because we wish to fill the Lord's day with praise and worship. We desire to enter into fellowship with God in his house as much as possible when given the opportunity.

Nor do God's people see this as a chore or as a mere requirement. They *want* to worship! It is their chief desire to enter into God's house with thanksgiving and prayer. It may be true that entering into God's house for worship twice a Sunday is tradition, but is it a good one or a bad one? God's people believe it is good, since it fulfills their desire to spend time in fellowship with their God.

Second, worshiping on the Lord's day is a requirement of the fourth commandment: "Remember the Sabbath day to keep it holy." The fourth commandment together with the other nine, though fulfilled by Jesus Christ, has not been destroyed (Matt. 5:17–19). The New Testament no longer worships on the seventh day according to Old Testament law. Having fulfilled the commandments through his work on the cross and in his resurrection, Christ fulfilled the Old Testament rest by ushering in the rest of the New Testament by his resurrection on the first day of the week. Through this work Christ has become the Lord of the Sabbath. This is why the church today speaks of our Sabbath as the Lord's day (Rev. 1:10). The first day of the week is sanctified by God. It is dedicated and consecrated by God himself to keep holy unto him.

This is accomplished by means of the worship of the church. God gives his church a day—a full day—to use in the worship of his name. He does not command his people to set aside an hour or two of the Lord's day to dedicate to the service of his name while the rest of the day is theirs. God commands his church to set aside this day to worship him.

This forms the basis of what the writer to the Hebrews enjoins God's people: "Let us hold fast the profession of our faith without wavering; (for he is faithful that promised) and let us consider one another to provoke unto love and to good works: *not forsaking the assembling of ourselves together*, as the manner of some is; but exhorting one another: and so much the more, as ye see the day approaching" (Heb. 10:23–25).

God commands us to keep the sabbath day holy because he knows we *need* this day to worship. The believer too recognizes that he needs time to enter into and enjoy fellowship with God for his spiritual strength. God uses this much-needed worship in church to keep his people's hearts set on the heavenly. Otherwise, it is so easy for the child of God to become so wrapped up in the here and now that he loses sight of God's covenant with him. Though he takes time out during the week for personal and family devotions, he realizes that he must also meet in God's house in order that his devotion to God and his kingdom may remain zealous. God understands this need and so commands us to keep the sabbath day holy unto him.

But what is it about worship in God's house that tugs at the heart of the believer? Why is it so special to go up into God's own house? Because the worship of the church itself is covenantal in nature. It is communication between Father and his children. How vital such communication is in order to remain strong in faith! God speaks to his children.

Those who sit in awe beneath his feet listen intently to what he tells them. He fills them with his word. They in turn, without drawing attention to themselves, respond to God's word and speak to him too.

They do this in an orderly and solemn way. They sit in the presence of God, after all. They heed God's command to them in Ecclesiastes 5:1–2, "Keep thy foot when thou goest to the house of God, and be more ready to hear, than to give the sacrifice of fools: for they consider not that they do evil. Be not rash with thy mouth, and let not thine heart be hasty to utter anything before God: for God is in heaven, and thou upon earth: therefore let thy words be few." A frenzied and clamorous worship service certainly is not biblical (1 Cor. 14:23, 33). True worship of God centers in God himself and his Son Jesus Christ. This is the way of God's covenant.

The worship centers in and surrounds the reading of God's word and the preaching. This must indeed take up the majority of the worship service. God's people sit at the feet of their good Shepherd, Jesus Christ, and listen to the word of God spoken by him.

Is it true that we hear Christ when the word of God is faithfully expounded and applied? This was certainly true in the Old Testament, when the prophets often spoke as if God himself were speaking to his people. How often we read in the prophecies of the Old Testament, "Thus sayeth the Lord."

But there are a couple of New Testament passages that speak of the same thing.

Paul wrote the words of Ephesians 4:20–21 to the Ephesian church made up, in the main, of Gentiles who had never seen or heard of Jesus Christ when he was on earth: "But ye have not so learned Christ; if so be that ye have heard him, and have been taught by him, as the truth is in Jesus."

How had these saints heard Jesus and been taught by him? Through the proclamation of the word given by those sent to them to preach. They heard the voice of the Head of the church through the preaching—not that Christ in some mystical and miraculous way suddenly stood before them in the person of the preacher, but that God chose to speak to them through the mouth of his ambassador whom he sent to speak to his saints on his behalf. The point is: during the worship service, God, through Christ, speaks to his people in the preaching of the word. God communicates with his people. This is an act of fellowship.

The various other elements of the worship service are secondary yet essential to fellowship with God. They are the response of God's children to what their Father says to them. They sing his praises. How joyful is the sound when God's people together lift up their voices and sing the praise of their God. When the voices of all of God's saints in the earth are joined together in song on the Lord's day, that sound is sweet in the ears of God, who takes delight in the praises of his people!

By means of prayer, God's children not only give praise to God but thank him for everything they are and possess. They also express their dependency on their Father, requesting of him all this is necessary for body and soul. They ask him to safeguard them from their enemies that would draw them away from him. They ask him to keep their souls when troubles befall them. Congregational prayer is one of the church's most intimate means of communication with the Father.

Then too, there is giving to the cause of the church. This is not an arbitrary act of worship. God's people recognize that everything they possess is given them from God. In love for God and his kingdom, they return to God a portion that their Father has given to them.

This interaction between God and his people in Christ during worship is of great benefit for God's people. It is true that the main purpose of worship is to render our praises to God. But there is a tremendous spiritual benefit for those who worship God in spirit and in truth.

Those who, on the one hand, view sitting in church as mere drudgery will walk away from church with no blessing at all. They will not be refreshed, strengthened, or encouraged. On the other hand, those who come to worship with a haughty attitude and view themselves as judges of the preaching and the preacher, those who are not really looking to be fed by the preaching, will also receive no blessing.

God's people must view the worship of the church on the Lord's day as their chief desire. They sing with Psalm 84:10, "A day in thy courts is better than a thousand. I had rather be a doorkeeper in the house of my God, than to dwell in the tents of wickedness." The worship of the church on the Lord's day must be most precious to those who share in God's covenant. These receive a blessing!

Chapter 11

The Gathering of God's Church

God's church has been in existence since the beginning of time. The body of the church is made up of elect believers. Abel was one of those believers. Hebrews teaches us that he offered his sacrifice to God *by faith*. Christ referred to him as "righteous Abel." A person is righteous before God only by faith.

Though Christ was not yet born in the Old Testament, and for that reason most of the time we speak of the church of *God* in the Old Testament, we could refer to the Old Testament church as the church of *Christ* too. After all, all of God's elect were chosen *in Christ* before the beginning of time. This is why Stephen in his defense before the council of the elders and scribes of the Jews in Acts 7:38 could make reference to the nation of Israel in the wilderness as "the church."

We make mention of this because from the beginning to the end of time, Christ *gathers* his church. With each new generation, God continues his covenant with his people in Christ. It is not our intent in this chapter to trace the line of God's covenant with his people since time's beginning. It is our intent, rather, to explain *how* God chooses to carry on his covenant and gather his church from one generation to the next.

Jesus describes his church in John 15:1–6 as a grapevine. "I am the vine, ye are the branches," he tells his church. We will use this figure of the grapevine to describe how God gathers his church throughout the ages.

When a husbandman plants a vineyard, he buries the root of a grape plant deeply into the ground. He then strings wire alongside it between two posts. As the grape plant grows, it sends forth its boughs or vines, which attach themselves to that wire. These vines grow along that wire, stretching themselves out from the plant of the grape bearing grapes. Each year the husbandman enters his vineyard and prunes out of the grapevine those branches that do not bear fruit. If he so chooses, he grafts other vines into that grape plant in their place in order that these branches, together with the existing branches, might continue to bear fruit.

At the beginning of time, God planted the grapevine of his elect church. Under God's care, that church sent forth its vine into the generations born into the church. It extended from one generation to the next, down through the wire of history.

For a while, that grape plant sent forth only one vine or bough. It was the vine of the nation of Israel, the generations of Abraham with whom God had established his covenant. The Psalmist in Psalm 80:9–11 describes how God planted this vine in Canaan after having delivered her from Egypt: "Thou preparedst room before it, and didst cause it to take deep root, and it filled the land. The hills were covered with the shadow of it, and the boughs thereof were like the goodly cedars. She sent out her boughs unto the sea, and her branches unto the river."

This vine continued throughout the natural generations of Abraham until the time of Jesus Christ. It was then that God graciously grafted branches into the vine of his church at the time of Pentecost. Using the figure of an olive tree, Paul in Romans 10 describes how the natural seed of Abraham were cut out of the vine to make room for the Gentiles.

This does not mean that the vine of the Old Testament church ceased. That church continued. There were many believing Jews that continued the vine of the Old Testament church. But since Pentecost, the grapevine of the church has sent forth many different branches, stretching down the wire of history from one generation to the next. These vines have been grafted into the vine of Christ's church at different times and from the various nations of this world. But they all belong to that one grapevine of Christ's church. These vines grow in the line of the continued generations of those who have been grafted in.

But there is a truth that may not be overlooked when viewing the gathering of Christ's church from one generation to the next. Jesus speaks of this in John 15:4, "Abide in me, and I in you. As the branch cannot bear fruit of itself, except it abide in the vine; no more can ye, except ye abide in me." Then in verse 6: "If a man abide not in me, he is cast forth as a branch, and is withered; and men gather them, and cast them into the fire, and they are burned."

With each new generation, Christ visits his vine. He prunes out of the vine of his church those branches that are a part of the church institute but who do not abide in him by a true and living faith. "They are not all Israel that are of Israel" (Rom. 9:6). At the same time, with each new generation, God grafts into the vine of his church other branches whose generations take their place in the church. This explains how God has gathered his church throughout the history of the New Testament.

Nor may we view this figure apart from God's covenant. Just as God gathers his church from one generation to the next, so also he establishes his covenant with that elect church in succeeding generations. God's fellowship with his people in Christ is passed along with each new generation that arises. Peter summarized it best in his sermon on the day of Pentecost: "For the promise is unto you, and to your children, and to all that are afar off, even as many as the Lord our God shall call" (Acts 2:39). Let's take note from this with whom God establishes his covenant.

First, Peter explains, the promise of the covenant is to you and your children! He was speaking in Acts 2 to the Jewish believers. In the Old Testament, God had established his covenant with his people from one generation to the next only *within the nation of Israel.* But Christianity was no longer the Judaism they had been taught.

These Jewish saints, no doubt, questioned in their own hearts: Would God continue to establish his covenant with them and their generations as he had done with the fathers of old? Would believing on Jesus Christ mean they were now going to be cut out of that covenant God had established with Abraham in his generations?

These saints were looking for the assurance that God would still dwell with them and be their God, and that they would be his people. Peter therefore reassures these Jewish believers that the covenant established of old with Abraham would still continue with them and with their children in their generations: the promise of that covenant is still with you and your children! With the new dispensation of God's covenant, the old covenant with Abraham is not discarded. God's covenant with Abraham continued with these Jewish believers in their generations. They could be reassured of that!

But the promise of God's covenant, Peter explains, is also with those that are afar off. Peter himself probably did not fully understand on that day what he had just spoken. The third sign that took place with the pouring out of the Spirit on the day of Pentecost was speaking in tongues. This sign pointed to the truth that the Spirit of Christ would be poured out on all flesh. All nations, peoples, and races of the earth would now receive the promise of salvation in Jesus Christ. God would eventually graft into the vine of his church and covenant every people of this earth. All the nations of the earth would be blessed in Abraham.

With the coming of Pentecost everything changed. Instead of establishing his covenant with one people and one nation of the earth, now God enters into fellowship with his chosen people from all nations. Unless we are so focused on our own little corner of the world with little interest in our confession, "I believe a holy, *catholic* (universal) church," we are able to see that this has become a reality today.

Peter adds the phrase "as many as the Lord our God shall call" (Acts 2:39). This applies not only to the second part of the verse, that is, "with all those that are afar off as many as the Lord our God shall call." It applies to the first part of that verse too: "unto you and your children ... as many as the Lord our God shall call."

God does not choose to save everyone in this world. He does not desire to save everyone. Though God publishes the call of the gospel without prejudice to all nations, only a few out of those nations are chosen and called by the Spirit and word unto salvation in Christ. The same is true, however, of children born to believing parents in the church. They too hear the call of the gospel externally within the sphere of the church, but God has chosen to work by his Spirit in the hearts only of some—perhaps many, yet only some—of these children. Election and reprobation cut through the heart of the church. Only those whom God has chosen unto salvation does he call with the saving call of the gospel.

These wondrous truths have much to say about the function of the church. If God gathers his church and establishes his covenant in the line of continued generations, the focus of the church lies in educating the children of the covenant. At the same time, if God gathers his church with each new generation by grafting others into his church and covenant, the focus of the church lies on mission work.

These two labors of the church do not contradict each other, nor are they mutually exclusive. The church must see to it "according to the demands of the covenant"[1] that its children are piously and religiously educated. On the other hand, the church is commanded by her Head, Jesus Christ, that she must go "into all the world and preach the gospel to every creature" (Mark 16:15). To overemphasize one to the exclusion or neglect of the other results in the church becoming lopsided in her labors, to the detriment of the life of the church.

God gathers in the line of continued generations. This truth is rooted in Scripture and in reality. This does not mean, however, that

---

1 Church Order of the Protestant Reformed Churches 21, in *The Confessions and the Church Order of the Protestant Reformed Churches* (Grandville, MI: Protestant Reformed Churches in America, 2005), 387.

believing children are dropped from heaven into the laps of believing parents. God is a God of means. God uses the church, first of all, to nurture the shoots that will spring forth out of the vine. The elders and pastors of the church must reveal to the children and youth that they are an important part of the church and covenant.

This is to be done, first of all, by instruction. Jesus commanded Peter to feed his lambs. The church must feed the children and youth of the church with God's word. Sermons that are always deeply dogmatic, with no application to the hearts and lives of children, will leave them hungry. God's word must be applied to the various struggles and temptations that confront the youth. Children and young people must sit under sound catechetical instruction. A pastor must take time while instructing the children and youth of the church to converse with them as if the children of the church were his very own children (which they are in a certain sense). The coming generation must learn of God's ways with his church (Bible history) and the truths that shape and mold our faith (doctrine).

The church must also encourage and admonish parents to spend time in the home with their children, carefully nurturing, loving, and disciplining them in the fear of God. Family visitation is a good time for elders and pastor to sit with the families of the church individually to discuss with them ways they can raise the next generation of believers. Sermons should be brought to bear on the place of the parents and children in the church. Parents must be encouraged to perform the vows they took at the time of the baptism of their children to raise their children, to the utmost of their power, in the truths of God's word. Emphasis must be placed by the church on the generations born into the sphere of the church and covenant.

It is true that with all of this, God does not choose to save all the children born into the church. The Spirit of Jesus Christ must be present and working in the hearts of our children. But God promises believing parents that the Spirit is present! Parents need not doubt that! God uses the weak but persistent means of the church and godly parents to raise up unto himself another generation of believers. These are new branches that shoot forth out of the vine and make their way into the future.

The church that neglects this will lose the next generation of believers. We mention this because many churches today neglect this in order to place most, if not all, the time and emphasis on reaching out to draw others in.

Those churches that are fiercely independent do not care about membership or caring for the sheep that become a part of their church. They are interested in marketing the gospel in an attempt to draw thousands in. They spend little energy on children. They are interested in drawing adults by means of the hype of a false gospel. These churches thrive for a generation and die out the next.

But there are also churches of conservative persuasion and good intentions that place all the emphasis on missions. The church institute tries to organize the members of the congregation into quasi-missionaries who spend their time leaving their family behind to go out to mission fields or canvassing neighborhoods in an attempt to find others that God may graciously graft into the vine of his church. The young people of the church are encouraged to visit mission fields.

Their motives are good. Their desire is to draw those lost in sin into the fold of the church and covenant. At times, however, so much emphasis is placed on missions and reaching out to the lost that forgotten is the time that pastors, elders, and parents need to spend with the children and youth of the church. Because the next generation is neglected, children of believers lose interest in the church. As a pastor of Reformed persuasion said to me in my small congregation, "My congregation is larger than yours, but you have children. I am afraid for the future of my church." We may not forget that God chooses to continue his covenant in that church where both church institute and the parents of that church commit time and effort to the training of their children.

God also chooses to gather his church with each new generation by calling, through the church, others from their unbelief unto faith. The church may not neglect her calling to evangelism and missions. Nor may these be given mere lip service.

Evangelism committees of individual congregations must be busy reaching out. The church institute, through her offices, must send out missionaries who are busy in foreign and domestic missions. God's people must support financially and with enthusiastic interest the mission programs of their denomination. There must be a genuine zeal to bring others unto faith, and ultimately membership in the church, by the preaching and personal witnessing.

As much as there is a desire to raise up children unto the Lord, so also must there be a desire to share the gospel of salvation with others. The denomination that hoards the blessed gospel to itself as if few others are worthy of it also eventually dies, no matter how much time, money, and effort is spent on the children and youth of the church.

Converts to the faith have a certain zeal for the truths of the gospel of grace that can be lacking in those who were born into the generations of the church. New believers bring to the church a genuine excitement for the truth the church has maintained, thus renewing the faith of those in the church who otherwise would have a tendency to take the gospel for granted. For that reason, mission work is an important aspect of the growth of the church and the extension of God's covenant from one generation to the next.

When the labor of the church centers in itself so that she fails to share the gospel with others, her work becomes lopsided in the other direction. She becomes self-centered. Her members see no reason for—and therefore shy away from—witnessing of their faith to others. Mission work wanes. Evangelism committees are at a loss for what to do. The church becomes reclusive. Money is funneled into the various causes of the church institute, but when it comes to mission work, people are content to pay the synodical budget for missions and leave it at that.

As one elderly woman said to me when I was a missionary, "I pray for you and your work on the mission field, but I give all my money to support the Christian education of my grandchildren." Indeed, Christian education is a noble cause, as we will find in the next chapter. But to the neglect of the preaching of the gospel in missions?

Ultimately this type of attitude ends up in suspicion of anyone outside of the bounds of the denomination. Pastors, elders, and finally the people become afraid that anyone outside of the church may pervert the truth. The church becomes separatist. The church and her members then become self-righteous and judgmental—not in doctrine, but in their attitude toward others.

Such churches assume the attitude of the Jews who boasted of the fact that they were the only chosen people of God. They had Abraham as their father; God's covenant was established with them; they were given the law and the prophets. Indeed, anyone outside of Israel was unclean. What an abomination that the gospel should be shared with the Gentiles!

A denomination that is not zealous in missions begins to reason in much the same way. We have the truth; God's covenant is established with us and our children; we carry with us the heritage of God's people. There are so very few outside our denomination that can be saved!

Such churches become ingrown. Suspicious eyes now turn toward fellow members of the church. People become judgmental in their attitude toward others in the church too. Gossip and slander soon take place. Quarreling and bitter words are spoken. Divisions and party strife begin in the church. "I'm a believer, but I'm not so sure about you!" Accusations are leveled against others.

Soon, the church becomes an undesirable place to live. Others will not join or, if they do, are soon driven out because they do not fit all the unspoken demands expected of them. The children we so carefully sought to nurture in the faith will become disillusioned with the church and will leave. The church slowly but surely dies in its life and labor.

Step back and take a hard look at the healthy, flourishing vine of God's church with which he establishes his covenant with each succeeding generation. Do you see its beauty? It is such a beautiful vine, the church! How has God kept it so plush and green while bearing fruit throughout the ages? He has done it by preserving his covenant in the line of the generations of the church. See how far down the vineyard the vine extends?

But God keeps his vine flourishing and green also by pruning from it the dead branches that bear no fruit. If he did not do that, then the vine would become barren and dry. Then God by his grace grafts other branches into that vine throughout the generations. Those born into the generations God uses to keep his church grounded in his covenant and the truths of God's word. Those grafted into the church lend zeal and enthusiasm to the life of the church.

—

Chapter 12

Educating Children of the Covenant

God's covenant is the foundation for establishing Christian schools. The Bible nowhere explicitly demands this. But that it is implied in Scripture is not difficult to ascertain. It is for that reason the Reformed Church Order in article 21 requires consistories to "see to it that there are good Christian schools in which the parents have their children instructed according to the demands of the covenant."[1]

It is important to note that this article does not require consistories to *establish* these Christian schools. Christ has not commissioned his church to educate children in secular studies. It is the calling and work of the church to preach and teach the gospel, not reading, writing, the sciences, and so on. But in their spiritual oversight of God's people under their care, consistories are called upon to encourage and even admonish parents to establish such Christian schools where children can be religiously educated.

Christian schools do teach the word of God as it applies to secular studies, but schools are not an arm of the church institute. Rather, Christian schools are parental in nature. They are an arm of the home. Schools are rooted in and find the reason for their existence in the family.

1 Church Order 21, in *Confessions and Church Order*, 387.

Scripture teaches us that God has given to *parents* the calling to instruct children in his covenant. The responsibility, therefore, of preparing children for their place and labor in this world belongs to them. We established this truth already when studying the relationship that exists between parents and children in the family. Scripture admonishes parents, for example, in Deuteronomy 6:4–9,

4. Hear, O Israel: The LORD our God is one LORD:
5. And thou shalt love the Lord thy God with all thine heart, and with all thy soul, and with all thy might.
6. And these words, which I command thee this day, shall be in thine heart:
7. And thou shalt teach them diligently unto thy children, and shalt talk of them when thou sittest in thine house, and when thou walkest by the way, and when thou liest down, and when thou risest up.
8. And thou shalt bind them for a sign upon thine hand, and they shall be as frontlets between thine eyes.
9. And thou shalt write them upon the posts of thy house, and on thy gates.

Believing parents are required by God, from the moment their children wake up to the time they fall asleep again, to teach them God's word as it applies to life. Certainly this is a time-consuming and difficult task!

What makes it more difficult is that with each passing generation, man's understanding of the laws of creation develops rapidly. In order for children to take their place in the various spheres of society, they must receive a thorough education. The advanced algebra and trigonometry learned today has far surpassed what was taught fifty years ago. Computer science, robotics, advanced technology in medicine, and more are all a common part of life and labor in today's world. These were not even heard of by earlier generations.

How can parents keep up with these changing trends in order to give their children an education that will stand them in good stead in their lives in this world? Even the basic courses in education, reading, writing, history, geography, and math require a great deal of time to teach in such a way that our children will learn all the facts profitably. Does a mother have time to teach all these while still caring for her infants and toddlers? Does a father have the time after earning a living for his family during the day?

Admittedly, there are some parents who are capable, disciplined, and organized enough to carry out this task at home. There are organizations that will help them out in this whole area of homeschooling. It can be done. But it takes much time and effort to educate children properly, especially if there are multiple children at different age levels. Most parents find that to keep pace with the duties in the home and teaching academics means they either allow other important matters in the home to "slip", or their children receive a shoddy education. For that reason, most parents turn to those who are properly trained to educate their children in the sphere of academics.

This is the reason for Christian schools from a practical point of view. But there is a spiritual reason for the formation of *Christian* schools, particularly of Reformed persuasion. God's precepts must be taught in *all* the instruction given to children by parents. Believing parents understand well that not only must their children be thoroughly trained in academics for their future, but these studies must also be taught in a distinctly Reformed way. Such parents live under the firm conviction of Proverbs 22:6, "Train up a child in the way he should go: and when he is old, he will not depart from it." If we as parents of God's covenant cannot teach our children at home, we insist that our children be trained in a Reformed Christian school.

If the task of educating children in their secular studies belongs to parents, believing parents ought to refuse the use of state-controlled schools. I have not studied the history of education in general or of Christian education more specifically, but perhaps a case could be made that a government should insist that its citizens be educated. For the advancement of learning and knowledge, the government must demand that its citizens receive a good education. No reasonable government wants its citizens to remain ignorant and backward. In the past when education was left up to families, many of them saw little need to educate their children beyond simple reading and arithmetic. If a nation desires to be powerful and influential in this world, its citizens must be educated.

But government has gone beyond simply demanding an education of its citizens. Now it also controls what is taught (and what is not) in schools. In our own land, we can be thankful that, under God's providential control, the government still allows parents to instruct their own children through the use of Christian day schools. However, the allurement of state-controlled schools is that the cost of such education is paid through the taxation of the citizens. Christian schools require large tuition payments in order to run these schools. These must be paid on top of the taxes paid to the government to run their schools, creating a hardship for many parents who send their children to a private Christian school.

At one time public (state-controlled) education may have seemed to be a reasonable option. Seventy-five years ago, many of the teachers were at least nominally "Christian" and at least taught good morals to children. Many children who attended the public schools came from families that had some sort of church membership, so the atmosphere in the schools did not seem to be so harmful to the life of Christian children. Besides, it was argued, sending our children into the public sector of education would give them an excellent opportunity to witness to others of their faith. They could be a light that might even overcome the darkness.

Forgotten was the Scripture, "Be not deceived: evil communications corrupt good manners"(1 Cor. 15:33). Perhaps this is more easily understood when translated into modern English. Paul writes, "Evil companions corrupt good habits." This is true in every sphere of life, but certainly believing parents ought to keep this in mind when tempted to send their children to public school.

There is a fundamental flaw in government-controlled education of children. The *government* controls the content of what is taught in the schools. Parents have no voice in the education of their own children. This is against the Scriptural mandate that *parents* must determine the spiritual direction of what is taught to their children. Allowing the children of God's covenant to be taught academically by unbelievers, by those who despise God and his commandments, is like giving our lambs to the wolves!

This has indeed proven to be the case in the slowly evolving development of public education. Students are not allowed to pray in public schools. Teachers in their instruction in the classroom may not be partial toward Christianity. The focus on instruction in public schools is not so much academics as behavior modification, that is, modifying the thinking and behavior of children to conform to the antichristian mindset of the government. Teachers and textbooks distort history. They openly teach sexual aberrations as normal behavior. Many public schools are filled with violence and immorality. Do Christian parents want their children exposed to the filth, the language, the violence of unbelieving classmates? Is this what they want for their children six or more hours a day?

Our youth find this out when they step out of the Christian high school into secular universities and colleges. They are immediately slapped in the face, as it were, by the openly godless, antichristian education that challenges them to question everything they are taught in the home and church.

But here is the point: parental schools are covenantal in nature! They are an extension of the home. They flow out of the Bible's instruction to parents to raise up their children in the fear of the Lord.

We need to be careful in our reasoning at this point, however. The same argument could be used for parochial schools, that is, church-run schools. We are writing on this important subject of educating our children under the general topic of God's covenant and life in the church. This might imply that schools are the work of the church institute rather than that of parents. Again, we stress that this is not the case. Rather, Christian education flows out of the *organic life of the church.* Families within the sphere of the church together see the need for the training of their children in academics from a distinctively Reformed perspective. Parents understand they are incompetent to do this on their own. As a result, they band together into an association or society in order to establish day schools where instruction is given according to their own doctrinal standards.

Schools are covenantal in this respect, then: they flow out of the organic life of the church. Schools are established according to the demands of God's covenant. God continues his covenant in the line of generations. These generations must be taught in God's ways. Believing parents set the standards for teachers to instruct their children in a way that those children would be taught in the home. Parents determine the content of what is taught in the classroom. In this way, parents, through the schools, are teaching their children.

The added benefit is that schools greatly assist in the life of the covenant found in the church. The children and youth of the church associate with fellow believers. They are able more freely to make companions of those who fear the Lord. These are able to bolster one another in the faith. Marriages often develop out of such relationships. Likewise, teachers assist in teaching in detail Bible history and the history of the church. Teachers require Scripture memorization and singing the songs of the church. All of this assists parents and the church in training up their children in the way they should go.

That being established, there are a few practical considerations and warnings that are necessary regarding the life of fellowship carried on in Christian schools.

First, teachers in the classroom stand in the place of parents. This is implied in *parentally* run schools. This makes our schools covenantal in character. Teachers do not hold a special office in the church. They are not fulfilling an official function on behalf of the church institute. But within the organic life of the church, believers use their talents and gifts for the advantage of other believers.

Teachers are hired to be surrogates of parents in the realm of the secular education of the children of believers. Those who desire to teach in the Christian school devote themselves to acquiring the proper education in order that they might help parents instruct their children in those subjects necessary to be fruitful in society and the church.

For that reason, the calling and work of an educator of the children of the covenant is weighty! Not only must teachers in the Christian school see to it that they are thoroughly prepared academically to teach, but they must also have a solid understanding of the Reformed faith. They must prepare themselves to teach every subject according to Scripture and the Reformed confessions.

A teacher who has little interest in Scripture will be ill-prepared to be a teacher in a distinctly Reformed Christian school. Each subject taught must be flavored with the word of God in order to teach the children of the covenant to live and breathe that word in their life and labors. That makes the calling of a teacher crucial! Believing parents rely on men and women of the church trained to teach in Christian schools to teach their children in their studies exactly what they are being taught in their home and their church.

Second, parents must instruct and admonish their children to honor and obey their teachers in the classroom just as they would their own parents. It is sad when parents pit their children against a teacher by always taking the side of their children over against the teacher.

What parent does not discipline their children in the home when that child walks in sin and disobedience? Do believing parents assume their children are without sin in the classroom or the hallways of the school? Of course not! Our children are sinners, and just as they are in need of admonition and discipline in the home, so also this may be true in the school.

A sure remedy for proper behavior in the classroom is for fathers to inform their children that if they get into trouble in school, they will be in trouble at home too. My father always told my teachers when I was young that if I was causing trouble in school, they had the right to discipline me. If they did, they also should inform him and I would be disciplined at home too. A double whammy! That kept my cantankerous nature in check!

The point is that parents and teachers must work harmoniously with one another. Teachers ought not to fear reprisal when, at parent/teacher conferences, they inform parents honestly that the behavior and application of their children to their studies needs improvement. Parents must not be hurt when someone other than themselves makes suggestions to help improve their children's behavior.

Teachers and parents are on the same side. Both have the interest of God's children in mind. When there is disagreement (and at times there is), then this too must be settled in a brotherly fashion between parents and teacher, without the children being aware of it. Children must always be taught that it is their duty to honor and obey their teachers in school just as they would their parents at home.

Third, when it is said that parents stand in the place of parents in the classroom, it does not mean that teachers replace parents in *their* calling to instruct their children. It is not the place of the school to do the work of a parent.

A Christian school ought not to follow the trends of the public school system. Many homes in our present society are dysfunctional. Domestic violence, abuse, single parent homes abound. The public schools have now begun to usurp the authority of parents. Teachers have become the eyes of social service agencies. Schools have taken on the role of counseling children, often giving them advice that parents would not give them themselves. Modern educators are instructed in how to modify the behavior of children to fit in with the worldly psychology of today. Christian schools ought not to follow after these worldly trends.

How easy it becomes for parents to relinquish to the school their calling to instruct their children faithfully and diligently in the home. Extra-curricular activities of the school often interfere with family worship. Individual study of the Bible and prayer is stressed, while little is said about the need for the family to gather each day to read and pray. Family worship disappears to be replaced by peer devotions.

Conversely, there can be so many school functions that time spent together in the home is sparse. The result is that children spend so much time with their classmates that they seldom go to parents for advice. They would rather gain advice from classmates or school counselors. When misbehavior arises with a group of friends outside the sphere of the school, people quickly blame the school for the trouble rather than the parents of these children or youth. Parents look to the school to fix it.

In reality, it is not the fault of the school, nor is it the school's calling to fix the problem. It is the fault of the home. Parents should be administering discipline in the home. When our children are distraught with the cares of life, anxious, and overwhelmed, the parents ought to be caring for these children in the home. Nothing can or ought to replace the loving care and counsel of fathers and mothers who know what is happening in the life of their children because they live and pray together. The school may not usurp nor be expected to replace the life of the covenant or the duties of parents toward their children in the home.

Fourth, a word of encouragement. Christian education is expensive! To send children to a school where sound education is given from a biblically Reformed perspective requires much of parents in the way of self-sacrifice. Parents need to be commended in their commitment to Christian education.

We live in a world dedicated to entertainment and recreation. Tens of thousands of dollars each year are channeled into the pursuit of enjoyment and fun. This is the only way the wicked seem to cope with life. In the home of families within the church, tens of thousands of dollars are instead routed into Christian schools. Some whom God has blessed with more will even give hundreds of thousands to Christian education. On the other side of the spectrum, committed parents will borrow money to see to it that their children are in those schools.

The maintenance of Christian schools with teachers dedicated to teaching from a Reformed perspective requires much sacrifice. Dedicated men serving on school boards volunteer much of their own personal time in order that schools might run efficiently. Parents of God's covenant are willing to make such a sacrifice. This is amazing! It reveals a genuine commitment to the cause of God's covenant in the line of the generations of the church.

May that same conviction be carried on in the next generation of believers and their children!

- Section Three -

God's Covenant and the Believer's Life in the World

—

Chapter 13

In, Not of, the World

What is the place of those who belong to God's covenant in this world, and more particularly, in the human race? How are we to live as a separate people dedicated and consecrated to serving God in this world of sin?

In Christ's intercessory prayer for his people in John 17, he defines the relationship of those given to him with those who are of the world. In John 17:14–18, Jesus prays concerning his people:

> 14. I have given them thy word; and the world hath hated them, because they are not of the world, even as I am not of the world.
> 15. I pray not that thou shouldest take them out of the world, but that thou shouldest keep them from the evil.
> 16. They are not of the world, even as I am not of the world.
> 17. Sanctify them through thy truth: thy word is truth.
> 18. As thou hast sent me into the world, even so have I also sent them into the world.

In short, God people are in the world but not of the world.

It is obvious from Jesus' use of the term "world" (*cosmos*) that he has in mind this present creation as it has come under the influence and power of unbelieving men. Adam, as the representative of the human race, received the mandate in Genesis 1:28 to subdue the earth and take dominion over it in order to develop this creation in the service of God, its Creator. When man fell into sin, he did not lose his dominion over creation, but instead of developing this creation in the service of God, he used it for his own advancement. Not only is this creation, therefore, under the curse of sin, but sinful, unbelieving man uses this creation in the service of his sin and unbelief. This is the world of which Jesus speaks in his prayer of John 17. He refers to the fallen human race, the world of sin and darkness.

Those whom God has given to Christ out of this world are God's elect people, chosen in Christ before the foundation of the world. These God gave to Christ in order that Christ might suffer and die to deliver them from sin and Satan. These are the members of the church and covenant of God.

Concerning these redeemed saints, Christ declares: "These are *in* the world" (John 17:11). Jesus explains in this short phrase that God is pleased to place the people of his covenant in the world. For this reason, Jesus petitions God: "I pray not that thou shouldest take them out of the world" (v. 15). From this it becomes clear that the people of God's covenant have a place in this world. Even more, God through Christ actually *sends forth* his people into this world with a purpose in mind. Jesus continues in his prayer: "As thou hast sent me into the world, even so have I also sent them into the world" (v. 18). Jesus sends them forth into this world to perform a certain function here.

The function of believers in this world does not require them to join hands with the world or become a part of the world. Jesus makes it clear in verse 14: "They are not of the world, even as I am not of the world." God sends his people into this world as representatives of his cause and kingdom, and therefore they are distinct from this world. They are not *of* this world. The wicked world is lost in the darkness of sin, while God's people are children of the light. This, then, becomes the axiom by which believers live: they are in the world but not of the world. When believers live with this truth before their minds, they will be able to navigate through this world of sin and darkness.

But what concretely is implied in the idea that you and I as believers are *in* this world? It is more than merely belonging to this present creation so that we rely on its air and food as all other creatures do. It means that God has sent forth his people to live together with people in this world, believer and unbeliever alike. We are a part of the society where God places us. We have a civil government that exercises authority over us. We are called to obey our magistrates by obeying the laws of the country where God has placed us. God's people are called to "honor the king" (1 Pet. 2:17). We must pay our taxes.

Many of God's people live in neighborhoods. They are called to interact with those neighbors and live peaceably with them (Rom. 12:18). The people of God's covenant need to work in this world to provide for themselves and their families. Often they must work side by side with an unbeliever, coordinating labors and communicating with him. Many times, God's people interact with others in the recreation they enjoy. They laugh and cheer with them at baseball games, waterparks, or lawn and garden shows. God's people are very much a part of the society and world where God places them. They are in the world.

But they are not *of* this world. They are not spiritually one with the wicked world of darkness, whose people walk in the way of sin and unbelief. Peter points out in 1 Peter 2:9, "Ye are a chosen generation, a royal priesthood, an holy nation, a peculiar people; that ye should shew forth the praises of him who hath called you out of darkness into his marvelous light." Those whom God has delivered from darkness into his light are now a peculiar—that is, a special, distinct—people, a people that God has separated unto himself. They have become the people of God's covenant.

Peter is drawing on Exodus 19:5, "Now therefore, if ye will obey my voice indeed, and keep my covenant, then ye shall be a peculiar treasure unto me above all people: for all the earth is mine." The same thing is found in Deuteronomy 7:6, "For thou art a holy people unto the Lord thy God: the Lord thy God hath chosen thee to be a special people unto himself, above all people that are upon the face of the earth." While we live in and interact with this present world of darkness, we are called to do so in faith, as those who are God's peculiar possession.

That we are in the world but not of the world is not a hard axiom to understand. But it takes faith to live it! The apostle Peter explains that one who is armed with the mind of Christ has ceased from sin: "that he no longer should live the rest of his time in the flesh to the lusts of men, but to the will of God. For the time past of our life may suffice us to have wrought the will of the Gentiles, when we walked in lasciviousness, lusts, excess of wine, revelings, banquetings, and abominable idolatries" (1 Pet. 4:2–3).

Peter describes accurately the excess of sin to which our present world is given. "Lasciviousness" means excess and refers to uncontrolled appetite for the pleasures of this world. "Lusts" refers to uninhibited sexual desires of every sort. Notice the phrase "excess of wine." Peter does not spell out here the sin of drunkenness, although this sin is included. He points out the sin of living for wine or alcohol so that at every turn, whether socially or at home, life revolves around that glass of wine or beer. "Revelings" is an old English word that means the same as our modern-day term "partying." By "banquetings," Peter means gluttony and drunkenness.

What an accurate description of the hedonistic society we find surrounding us in this world of sin! Peter explains that was true of our past life. That is no longer true of the believer's life in this world now. Why? Because though we find ourselves in this world of sin, we are not of this world of sin. We have been delivered from the sins of this world. These sins ought no longer to characterize believers! We will pursue this more in another chapter.

At times, the believer who is weary with his battle against sin wonders why God, having saved him, leaves him in this world of unbelief. But we must remember what Christ says in John 17: he sends us forth into this world. Christ has a purpose for us in this world. Those who belong to God's covenant must be in this world because they are called to be a light in the midst of the darkness of sin. They are called to be witnesses to this world of sin of the work of God's grace in their lives, delivering from that sin.

Jesus teaches us this truth in his sermon on the mount: "Ye are the light of the world. A city that is set on a hill cannot be hid. Neither do men light a candle, and put it under a bushel, but on a candlestick; and it giveth light unto all that are in the house. Let your light so shine before men, that they may see your good works, and glorify your Father which is in heaven" (Matt. 5:14–16).

Peter states it a bit differently in 1 Peter 2:11–12, "Dearly beloved, I beseech you as strangers and pilgrims, abstain from fleshly lusts, which war against the soul; Having your conversation honest among the Gentiles: that, whereas they speak against you as evildoers, they may by your good works, which they shall behold, glorify God in the day of visitation."

Christ sends forth his people into this world to testify of him and his salvation. By means of their godly lives, the wicked are reproved for their sin. On the other hand, God uses this testimony to draw others unto faith and repentance in Jesus Christ.

This is one reason we are placed by Christ in this world.

A second reason Christ sends his people into this world is to develop it in the service of his name. Man in Paradise was given the mandate to subdue and replenish the earth in the service of its Creator. The believer still has this calling, even after the fall—*especially* after the fall. While the wicked of this world have made great strides in developing this creation, it is all in the service of man. Those of God's covenant discover the laws of nature and use these to advance the kingdom of God. We live in this world and perform our labors with the goal always in mind that we must redeem the times on behalf of Christ's cause and kingdom in this world.

Believers too enter into the various spheres of life and labor. Belonging to God's covenant does not prohibit the believer from entering into technology, medicine, politics, law, business, trades, and much more. In doing so, however, he realizes that in all of these spheres of labor, he is a representative of God's covenant and will therefore utilize these labors to promote the cause of Christ in this world.

For that reason, it would be wrong for God's people to separate themselves from society and life in the world. There is a call to *spiritual* separation, of course, but it is not a call to world flight.

The Anabaptists during the time of the Reformation believed that belonging to the kingdom of Christ gave them the right to ignore civil governments and form their own communities with their own set of laws. When civil authorities demanded that they obey the laws established by the country these communities were in, they refused. As a result, many Anabaptists were put to death for rebellion against the government. They, in turn, believed they were being martyred for the sake of Christ and his kingdom. They were wrong!

Believers are in this world, a part of the communities and societies in which they are found, and that, according to the command of Christ. Many of the Anabaptists fled Europe and settled in America, where there is freedom of religion in order to pursue their world flight. We find these in the Amish and Mennonite communities still in existence today. Their quiet lifestyle ought not to deceive us. They deny what Christ requires of us as his children: to be in the world, yet to remain a distinct people that does not conform itself to the world.

Bearing this principle of Scripture in mind, we understand our calling as God's children as we lead our lives in this world.

—

Chapter 14

Loving the Neighbor

Crucial to the life of the believer in this world is the keeping of the second table of the law. The Heidelberg Catechism in question and answer 93 points out that this table of the law presents us with the duties we owe our neighbor. Nor is this foreign to the life we as God's people lead within the covenant.

We learn in Exodus 34:28 that the ten commandments are the "words of God's covenant." These words of God's covenant are written upon the fleshy tables of our hearts. They become part and parcel of the life of the believer in the home, the church, and the world.

Nor may we ignore the truth that the only way to keep God's law is by loving God and the neighbor. A mere outward conformity to the law of God means nothing to God. The believer keeps the commandments only by loving God and the neighbor. This means I must love my neighbor in the home, the church, *and the world*. I must love my neighbor in the world with heart, mind, and strength.

For that reason, some question whether the neighbor includes the wicked people of this world. They insist that the only true neighbor of the believer is another believer. The wicked are our enemies, and therefore the second table of the law does not apply to our lives in this world. We may not love our ungodly neighbor. We may love only those who are brothers and sisters in the church.

These same people remain aloof from their unbelieving neighbors, refusing to talk with them except when necessity demands it of them. They have a condescending attitude toward those outside of their church. They may even go so far in their self-righteousness as to exclude themselves from contact with those who are of a different church.

This conception of the neighbor is faulty for two reasons, according to Scripture. First, it is based on an erroneous conception of what constitutes a neighbor. Second, it is founded on a misconception of love.

Jesus teaches us the proper understanding of who our neighbor is in his parable of the Good Samaritan in Luke 10:29–37. A certain Jewish lawyer, who desired to justify himself, asked Jesus, "Who is my neighbor?" Jesus pointed out in this parable that the question is not really "Who is my neighbor?" as much as "To whom am I a neighbor?"

A man was robbed along the wayside from Jericho to Jerusalem. He was beaten and left for dead. In time, a priest and a Levite passed along the way and, instead of stopping to help the man, crossed over to the other side of the road, ignoring his need. But a certain Samaritan man passed by, took compassion on this man, nursed him to health, and then left money behind at an inn for his continued care. Who was this injured man's neighbor? Surely not the priest or the Levite. It was that Samaritan man. Why? Because he, seeing the need of a stranger, was willing to show compassion and kindness to him.

The same is true of a believer. The love of God is shed abroad in our hearts! The fruits of the Spirit have been worked in us. The fruit of the Spirit in us is love, peace, longsuffering, gentleness, goodness, and faith. We receive the command in Colossians 3:12, "Put on therefore, as the elect of God, holy and beloved, bowels of mercies, kindness, humbleness of mind, meekness, longsuffering."

If indeed God has shed his love abroad in the believer's heart, then that believer always acts out of that love. When a person around him is in need in this world, whether a believer or unbeliever, the child of God is always ready and willing to help. When an ungodly neighbor comes to me and asks me if he can use my lawnmower, am I going to refuse and say, "Because you do not believe in God, I will not help you?" No, I will do good to him. If an unbeliever mourns the loss of a wife or child, will I callously ignore him without testifying to him of the comfort that can be found in Christ?

There is no doubt that the closest of neighbors are those who are one with us in the church. In fact, since we deal with them more than anyone else, the commandments of the second table of the law apply more readily to them.

But the neighbor must be defined as all those whom God has placed in our path as we walk through this life. My neighbor is not necessarily that person on the other side of the earth that does not cross my path in any way. That can happen too, we realize, given the modern age of technology and travel. But my neighbor is that person with whom I come in personal contact.

My enemy? Yes, my enemy too. Jesus' teaching on this matter is clear. We read in Matthew 5:43–48,

> 43. Ye have heard that it hath been said, Thou shalt love thy neighbor, and hate thine enemy.
> 44. But I say unto you, Love your enemies, bless them that curse you, do good to them that hate you, and pray for them which despitefully use you, and persecute you;
> 45. that ye may be the children of your Father which is in heaven: for he maketh his sun to rise on the evil and on the good, and sendeth rain on the just and on the unjust.
> 46. For if ye love them which love you, what reward have ye? do not even the publicans the same?
> 47. And if ye salute your brethren only, what do ye more than others? do not even the publicans so?
> 48. Be ye therefore perfect, even as your Father which is in heaven is perfect.

This neighbor we are commanded to love. Love. Now, that is a word misused and abused by the wicked world and even many in the church! Few people today know what true love is. Most people view it as sensual and even erotic. Others define it as a feeling or affection a person can fall into and out of as quickly as one's feelings change.

But the truth of Scripture is that God is love! There is no true love apart from God. In this love, God sent his only begotten Son, the Son of his love, to death for us who were his enemies (Rom. 5:6–8). God gave his Son for us. Likewise, Christ, in love for God's people, gave of himself for us when he laid down his life for us.

As a result, God has shed abroad in the hearts of his children that same love. That love is not a feeling that comes and goes. It is rooted in our knowledge of God and who he is. It is rooted in Jesus Christ who dwells in us. That love we have for God and our Savior becomes the foundation of the love we show towards others. We love others with the love of God that dwells in us. Such love binds us together with others of like faith. The bond we share together with Christ and his bride, the church, is so firm that even if father or mother forsake us, even if a child rebels against God, our love for the church does not waver.

But this same love we have for God and our Savior motivates us in our dealings with the wicked people of this world. Obviously, this love does not unite us with them. We are not drawn to them as we are to those who believe as we do. In fact, in the next chapter we will examine the opposite aspect of our relationship with the wicked. We do not join with the wicked, since the love we must show them is holy and pure while they are not.

So then how does our love reveal itself toward our neighbor? We live in a world filled with hatred and strife. There is horrible unrest in society. The governments of this world are becoming more antichristian. The number of those who faithfully represent God's kingdom and covenant is becoming smaller. How do we live in the way of love in a world filled with hatred? What ought to be the reaction of those who live in fellowship with God over against those who despise God and his fellowship?

First of all, we love the neighbor by keeping the second table of the law. We walk in the way of the book of the covenant: God's word and commandments. We keep the fifth commandment: we honor those whom God has placed in authority over us in society. We obey the sixth commandment: we live peaceably with all men showing "patience, peace, meekness, mercy, and kindness towards him, and, so far as we have power, to prevent his hurt; also, to do good even unto our enemies."[1] We honor the seventh commandment: we love our neighbor by living chaste and holy lives in marriage as well as in single life. We obey the eighth commandment: we are honest in our dealings with others, or, as the Heidelberg Catechism in question and answer 11 teaches us, we promote their advantage in every instance we can or may. We keep the ninth commandment: in all our dealings with our neighbors, we love the truth, speak it uprightly, confess it, and defend their honor and good character.

The tenth commandment is unique. It summarizes the other commandments and reveals that the keeping of the law is a matter of the heart. Covetousness is the strong desire to possess something that someone else has. This sin underlies all our sin: a desire for my neighbor's position, a desire for another person's spouse, a desire for his possessions, a desire to slander his good name. Covetousness at root is selfishness and narcissism. It is the attitude that thinks that I may have and deserve to have what my neighbor has. As members of God's covenant, we must flee from such sin. We must reveal our love for God and our salvation by loving our neighbor.

Our conversation in this world must be in all honesty and godliness. Peter gives us this summons in 1 Peter 2:12 and 15: "Having your conversation honest among the Gentiles: that, whereas they speak against you as evildoers, they may by your good works, which they shall behold, glorify God in the day of visitation.... For so is the will of God, that with well doing ye may put to silence the ignorance of foolish men."

Second, loving the neighbor requires that we leave a godly witness

---

1 Heidelberg Catechism Q&A 107, in Schaff, *Creeds of Christendom*, 3:347.

in our dealings with him. Negatively, this means we do not deal with our neighbor in an underhanded way, attempting to take advantage of him. God's word is clear. We must be "providing for honest things, not only in the sight of the Lord, but also in the sight of men" (2 Cor. 8:21). Or again, "Having your conversation honest among the Gentiles..." (1 Pet. 2:12). We must be honest in our speech, in our labors, and in our conduct with others.

A godly witness is letting our light so shine before men that they can see Christ shining in us. We must not be ashamed of who we are. We must hold high the banner of Jesus Christ. This does not mean we are showy or sanctimonious in our Christianity. We simply live and speak as those in whom the Spirit of Christ dwells. Nor are we afraid to give an answer concerning what we believe to those who ask us about the hope that dwells in us (1 Pet. 3:15). Certainly we are witnesses of the cause of Christ in a dark world of sin and unbelief. This witness cannot be given if we lead a reclusive life that shuts out the unbeliever from our dealings.

Third, loving the neighbor will also reveal itself in the way of hospitality. Abraham entertained angels unaware. He was sitting in the door of his tent and three strangers appeared. He invited them to rest under the shade of a tree, brought them water to drink, bread and meat to comfort their hearts, and water to wash their feet. These men were strangers! The Levitical law required this love: "Love ye therefore the stranger: for ye were strangers in the land of Egypt (Deut. 10:19).

Does this mean that I, as a believer, can dine with an unbeliever? May I go to his house and visit him or invite him to my house to visit with him? I surely may! Jesus did! We read in Mark 2:15, "And it came to pass, that, as Jesus sat at meat in his house, many publicans and sinners sat also together with Jesus and his disciples: for there were many, and they followed him."

The self-righteous scribes and Pharisees condemned Jesus for this action. But these sinners had come to Jesus to learn the way of salvation. At times, this may be true in the life of a believer too. God's people do not make unbelievers their companions. We will learn more about this in the next chapter. But certainly if my neighbor desires to sit down and talk to me, I must be both approachable and friendly.

Finally, loving the neighbor requires us to walk in humility in a proud world. This goes without saying. We too were enemies of God who, by his grace, were taken into his family. We do not merit or deserve to be members of his covenant and cause in this world. God has adopted us as his own children freely by his grace, though we were no better than the unbeliever who is still lost in his unbelief.

Ought we not to act in humility toward the unbelieving neighbor? Does not this humility require of us gentleness and kindness? These are gifts of the Spirit that God has worked in our hearts. As God's children, we show kindness to the wicked as well as the righteous. We deal with men gently.

God's people are *not* militaristic. As this wicked world increases in its hatred for God's cause and kingdom, believers do not riot to maintain their "religious rights." They do not take up arms against government. The battle they fight is a spiritual one. This is God's word in 2 Timothy 2:24–26 for dealing with those who oppose the gospel: "The servant of the Lord must not strive; but be gentle unto all men, apt to teach, patient, in meekness instructing those that oppose themselves; if God peradventure will give them repentance to the acknowledging of the truth; and that they may recover themselves out of the snare of the devil, who are taken captive by him at his will."

It is true that those who opposed Timothy could very well have been belligerent members in the church rather than outside of the church, but the attitude we exude toward all who oppose the gospel, whether in the church or outside of it, must always be that of patience and meekness. "Be gentle unto all men."

In these last times, we need to be reminded that our goal or end is not to establish the kingdom of Christ on earth. It is to strive to enter into the kingdom of heaven. That requires of us spiritual stamina. It requires wisdom and understanding of the word of God. It requires that we love God and the neighbor.

All of this hinges on the one important reality of the believer's life: he belongs to his faithful Savior, Jesus Christ, who has purchased him with his blood. By God's grace, he shares in the blessed life of communion and favor of God. The believer strives in this life to enter into the perfection of that fellowship in heaven. That is how the kingdom of Christ is won.

—

Chapter 15

Living Antithetically

The last chapter may have left some of us confused. The law commands us to love the neighbor. Jesus tells us to love and pray for our enemies. Scripture teaches us to live peaceably with all men, to show kindness and hospitality even to the stranger.

But this does not seem to harmonize with other Scriptures that teach us the opposite. For example, John teaches us in 1 John 2:15–16, "Love not the world, neither the things that are in the world. If any man love the world, the love of the Father is not in him. For all that is in the world, the lust of the flesh, and the lust of the eyes, and the pride of life, is not of the Father, but is of the world."

James strongly exhorts God's people in James 4:4, "Ye adulterers and adulteresses, know ye not that the friendship of the world is enmity with God? whosoever therefore will be a friend of the world is the enemy of God."

How can we be called to love the neighbor and yet at the same time not to love the world? The two seem mutually exclusive. This needs a proper explanation.

After the fall of man into sin, God spoke what has become known as the mother promise. The words he spoke were actually directed toward Satan, yet they contain the promise of a coming Savior: "And I will put enmity between thee and the woman, and between thy seed and her seed; it shall bruise thy head, and thou shalt bruise his heel" (Gen. 3:15).

The result of the fall would be that two distinct and opposing peoples would develop in this world: the seed of the woman and the seed of the serpent. The seed of the woman is the church that belongs to Christ since the beginning of time. The seed of the serpent is the unbelieving, reprobate world that is given over to the power of sin and Satan.

Between these two seeds God puts enmity, that is, animosity and hostility. This was revealed already in the first two sons of Adam and Eve. Wicked Cain murdered his righteous brother Abel because God had accepted Abel's sacrifice of faith and not Cain's sacrifice of works.

The point is that one of the consequences of man's fall into sin is a spiritual separation between those who believe and the ungodly who, in unbelief, remain hardened in their sin. When children were born to Adam and Eve, God began to work out his sovereign decree of election and reprobation in time. God created a spiritual chasm, a marked separation between his elect and the reprobate.

This is clearly pointed out in 2 Corinthians 6:14–16, "What fellowship hath righteousness with unrighteousness? and what communion hath light with darkness? And what concord hath Christ with Belial? or what part hath he that believeth with an infidel? And what agreement hath the temple of God with idols?"

God calls his elect out of the darkness of unbelief and the disobedience of the world yet lost in sin. God's people are the children of the light as opposed, therefore, to the children of the darkness. Light and darkness are opposites. There is no communion between them.

God's elect are made righteous in the blood of Jesus Christ. The reprobate man and woman of this world are yet lost in their wickedness. Righteousness and unrighteousness are opposites that can have no fellowship with each other.

God's people are the followers of Jesus Christ. He is their Lord. The wicked follow after their prince, Satan. These form two spiritual camps that are opposed to one another. One cannot be a part of both camps at the same time. What part does one who believes have with an unbeliever?

Unbelief is blindness, faith is sight. These are opposites. We either see in faith or are blind in unbelief.

The last question Paul asks in these verses is: "What agreement has the temple of God with idols?" The church in this world is a spiritual house built to offer spiritual sacrifices acceptable to God. God dwells in her. The church is the temple of God, therefore. The reprobate also are a spiritual house—a house built to serve the idols of this world, the lust of the flesh, the lust of the eye, and the pride of life. One cannot be a stone in God's temple and a stone in the temple of idols.

No believing student of the Scripture will deny the existence of a huge spiritual gulf between those who are members of God's covenant in this world and those who are not.

The Bible speaks of two spiritual kingdoms that develop side by side throughout the history of the world: the kingdom of Christ and the kingdom of man, with Satan at its head. From the beginning of time until the end there is a constant war between the two. The kingdom of man repeatedly raises its ugly head to destroy the church of Jesus Christ. It has done so in the past and is doing so at present.

Satan and his ally, the wicked world, attempt to lure the members of God's covenant and kingdom into their kingdom either by force or by temptation. On the other side of the battle is the church. The members of God's covenant delight in fellowship with God and therefore despise fellowship with the unfruitful works of darkness.

In hatred against sin and Satan, the church goes forth into the world to preach the gospel in order that the wicked "may recover themselves out of the snare of the devil, who are taken captive by him at his will" (2 Tim. 2:26). The church attempts to rescue the citizens of this world from imminent destruction. There is a spiritual battle going on! This is the result of the spiritual enmity God himself places between the seed of the woman and the seed of the serpent.

The members of God's cause and covenant must always carry this important truth in their hearts and live with it before their minds: we do *not* belong to a brotherhood of all men! We are not *of* this world.

It is true that all mankind in Adam has fallen into the deep way of sin. We with the wicked deserve to perish in that sin. That humbles the believer. But we have been delivered from sin and its guilt through the precious blood of our Savior. We belong, therefore, to the brotherhood of believers. We are members of the body of Christ and therefore belong to the fellowship of God. We are the children of his family. That sets us apart from the wicked of this world.

This means that we may not walk with unbelievers. God asks us in Amos, "Can two walk together, except they be agreed?" (3:3). We sing with the Psalmist,

Their sorrows shall be multiplied
Who worship ought but thee;
I share not in their offerings,
Nor join their company!
The Lord is mine inheritance.[1]

The believer sins when he or she seeks the companionship of the ungodly. The Bible repeatedly draws a sharp contrast between the life and place of the believer in this world and that of the unbeliever. This contrast is best described by a word not often heard anymore today: "antithesis." This term means "direct and unequivocal opposite." The antithesis of the light is darkness. The antithesis of the truth is the lie.

The word "antithesis" stands opposed to all *synthesis*, a blending together of two different ideas or lifestyles. For example, some seek to synthesize the creation account with evolution. Some try to synthesize sovereign predestination with a love of God for every man. But the two cannot be blended together. They are direct and unequivocal opposites of one another. They stand in antithesis to one another. Creation is the truth; evolution is the lie. Sovereign predestination is the truth; God's love for every man is a lie. The truth and the lie stand in antithesis to one another.

---

1 No. 27:3-4, in *The Psalter*.

So also those who belong to the family of God's covenant stand over against those who still dwell in the darkness of sin and unbelief. In Ephesians 4:17–19, Paul says,

> 17. This I say therefore, and testify in the Lord, that ye henceforth walk not as other Gentiles walk, in the vanity of their mind,
> 18. having the understanding darkened, being alienated from the life of God through the ignorance that is in them, because of the blindness of their heart:
> 19. who being past feeling have given themselves over unto lasciviousness, to work all uncleanness with greediness.

We were lost in the same darkness of sin as the reprobate man. But God has been gracious! He has delivered us from that darkness and given light to our eyes. We are now a spiritually different people than the wicked of this world. God has set us apart and consecrated us unto the service of his name. We represent his cause and kingdom in this world.

This has everything to do with the way we conduct ourselves. The church of Jesus Christ today must examine itself closely. Is this antithesis evident in the lives of its members? Or has the church today begun to look like the unbelieving world?

Romans 1:29–31 lists the evils into which God has given men of reprobate minds. Among them are fornication, murder, maliciousness, disobedience, and backbiting. Paul not only points out God's judgment on those who commit these sins, but also condemns those who "have pleasure in them that do them" (v. 32). The wicked not only commit these sins; they are entertained by them. How often do we, who have been delivered from such sin and now live in fellowship with the holy God, take pleasure in watching or listening to the wicked in their sins?

Living the antithesis does not consist in following a set of rules. It is not a matter of carefully following the mandates of the church, but then using the life of liberty to indulge in the ways of the world. It is not a matter of keeping company with believers when at church or school, and then enjoying the companionship of unbelievers when out of sight of other believers.

Living the antithesis is a matter of the heart. That is where the child of God has been changed. The heart is no longer conformed to this world but is transformed by the renewing of our mind. There is nothing more the believer desires than the friendship and fellowship of God. Well, he who desires to be a friend of God must view the world as his enemy (James 4:5).

The principle of the antithesis manifests itself in two ways.

First, God's people must seek to be companions with God's people. The young Psalmist writes in Psalm 119:63, "I am a companion of all them that fear thee, and of them that keep thy precepts."

Life in this world requires interaction with unbelievers. Unless we are reclusive, we meet them in our neighborhoods, while on vacations, and especially in the workplace. The unbeliever is not some freak of nature. Although some may immediately repel us by their foul language, vulgar conversation, and brazen disregard for anything decent, such is not true of many others. They seem to be normal people with mutual interests. They have similar joys and problems in life. They may have sparkling personalities that are easy to warm up to. Unbelievers often can be very attractive on the outside. The ungodly of this world are normal human beings.

But there is a huge *spiritual* gulf between those who belong to God's covenant and kingdom in this world and those who do not. We love God. We find our all in Jesus Christ. We have been delivered from the horrible bondage of sin and Satan. Our goal is the kingdom of heaven. None of this is true of the ungodly of this world—even of many who *claim* to love God. The very heartbeat of their lives is essentially different from ours.

For that reason, we make friends of God's people. Believers belong to the family of God. They are brothers and sisters in the same household. They are God's friends together. They are members of the body of Christ together.

There is every reason in the world therefore to seek out those who, together with us, love God and have the same goals as we do spiritually. Not only do we make believers our friends, but we make them our life's mates, our husband or wife.

Certainly if we may not make companions of unbelievers, we may not seek a husband or wife from among unbelievers. The Bible is very clear on this. In Genesis 6 we learn of the great wickedness that developed in the earth prior to the Flood. "All flesh had corrupted his way on the earth" (v. 12). The beginning of that chapter reveals how the world had developed to this stage. "The sons of God saw the daughters of men that they were fair; and they took them wives of all which they chose" (v. 2). Young men of the church, men who belonged to the sphere of God's covenant, were attracted to the unbelieving women of the world. They married them, and they produced children of unbelief who became mighty men of the world. Not of the church, mind you, but of the world. In this way, wickedness spread throughout the earth, and the church dwindled to eight souls.

Prior to their entering into the land of Canaan, Moses commanded the nation of Israel to destroy the heathen nations. They should make no covenant with them. "Neither shalt thou make marriages with them; thy daughter thou shalt not give unto his son, nor his daughter shalt thou take unto thy son. For they will turn away thy son from following me, that they may serve other gods: so will the anger of the LORD be kindled against you, and destroy thee suddenly" (Deut. 7:3–4).

After the nation of Israel conquered the land of Canaan and settled into the houses and fields God had given them in the land, we learn in Judges 3 that Israel actually dwelt among the heathen nations of Canaan that they failed to destroy. This is what happened: "And they took their daughters to be their wives, and gave their daughters to their sons, and served their gods. And the children of Israel did evil in the sight of the LORD, and forgat the LORD their God, and served Baalim and the groves" (Judges 3:6–7). Sinful intermarriages between the members of the church and the people of this world always have led to the demise of the church.

The refusal to form bonds with the unbeliever does not contradict the command of God's word to love our neighbor. There is a difference between showing oneself cordial and friendly toward a neighbor and walking together with him in his ungodly lifestyle. There is a difference between helping a neighbor, and even sympathizing with him, and walking in spiritual union with him. There is even a difference between sitting together with him to counsel him in God's word and superficially dining with him strictly for entertainment. What would happen to our relationship with an ungodly person if we were to live and witness to him of our life in Christ? It would either by God's grace lead him to the cross, or the relationship would soon die since he would find little in common with us.

It is true that godly relationships have developed out of a young man or woman finding a spouse outside of the realm of the covenant. This is not a rule, but an exception; yet it can happen. Usually, however, this relationship began with a young Christian openly displaying and talking about his or her faith with the other. Neither was marriage proposed until the unbeliever understood his or her sin and the need for the cross of Jesus Christ, as well as the great truths of grace.

This, then is the first way we live the life of the antithesis: we seek to make friends of God's people who openly confess their sin and need for the cross of Christ

A second way we are called to live the antithesis is by rejecting the godless principles, philosophy, psychology, and lifestyle of the wicked. What motivates a young man or woman to seek out the fellowship of an unbeliever? What do they share with each other that becomes a common bond between them? Certainly it is not the life of a Christian! Should a son or daughter of the church seek the companionship of the unbeliever on the basis of the lifestyle of the unbeliever?

This is why the believer's life in this world must be that of the antithesis! Most of the lifestyle of the wicked, most of the secular reasoning of "professionals" today, comes via entertainment and the media. This is why we intend to devote a chapter to the life of the believer and entertainment.

The child of God's covenant must seek to live according to the standard of God's word. That must be his guide in life. Where do we turn for life in the home? To God's word! How do we view marriage? What is the calling of a husband and wife in marriage? How do we raise children? How do we nurture children when they are toddlers or when they become teenagers? The answers are found in God's word. We do not seek out the worldly wisdom of secular psychologists or family therapists to find the answer to these questions. We look to God's word for answers.

What is our calling in or relationships with others in society or the church? We do not seek answers from those who are filled with their own good advice, life's experiences, or feelings, but never make reference to what God's word teaches. We look to God's word and good, sound, biblical writing that roots advice in the word of God. The life of Christ in us attracts us to what God tells us and not what the wicked in their unbelief tell us.

That is living the life of the antithesis. We say yes to what God tells us in his word and no to the wicked of this world. We live a life of spiritual separation from the unbelief of this world. We belong to God's cause and covenant in this world. We are a distinct and holy people, who are consecrated to serving God and fleeing the ways of wickedness. We are spiritually different from the world. What do others see in us?

Chapter 16

The Believer in the Workplace

Much of the life of a believing man is spent in the workplace earning a living for himself, his family, and the church. Parents must teach their sons to be good providers for their families and the church.

Parents who think that youth is a time for fun and irresponsibility do their sons and daughters a disservice. Already little children in the home must be taught to labor on behalf of the family. They may not be selfish but must understand that they have an obligation toward the family unit.

When they come to years of discretion, young men and women must be taught to work, not for the frivolities of life, but in order to contribute to the family and church. In an age of prosperity, parents begin to think that children are entitled to receive everything from their parents without working for it themselves. That is wrong. Such thinking on the part of parents will result in a generation that is selfish, using the fruit of their labors only for their own pleasure.

Paul's command to the church in Ephesians 4:28 is, "Let him that stole steal no more: but rather let him labor, working with his hands the thing which is good, *that he may have to give to him that needeth.*" The emphasis of this passage may not be overlooked. We must labor, not for ourselves, but for the person who needs what we earn.

Obviously, our family will have needs. We labor to meet those needs. But the church also has great need. We labor to support the church. The poor we have with us always, Jesus says. They too have a need. We labor to support them as well.

Children must be taught to work. Children must be taught that the money they earn is not to be used selfishly for themselves but for those who are in need.

Likewise, this passage in Ephesians 6 teaches the believer to work *hard.* Employees may not steal. They may not waste their time on the job. This can be done by shoddy work, sluggishness, or taking breaks not scheduled by the employer (perhaps to check our cell phones to answer emails and texts).

The Bible condemns laziness. The well-known proverb of Solomon comes to mind:

> 6. Go to the ant, thou sluggard; consider her ways, and be wise:
> 7. which having no guide, overseer, or ruler,
> 8. provideth her meat in the summer, and gathereth her food in the harvest.
> 9. How long wilt thou sleep, O sluggard? When wilt thou arise out of thy sleep?
> 10. Yet a little sleep, a little slumber, a little folding of the hands to sleep:
> 11. so shall thy poverty come as one that travelleth, and thy want as an armed man. (Prov. 6:6–11)

Paul's simple instruction to the Thessalonian church must be heeded today too: "If you don't work, you don't eat!" (see 2 Thess. 3:7–12). When a man labors hard with his hands or his mind (or both), then the Lord blesses the labors of his hands. With the fruit of his labor—that is, the money he earns—the believer then gives to meet the needs of his family and the church. That is his duty.

But laboring in this world requires a man to be *in* the world. In fact, a large share of his day is spent in the world eking out a living. He labors in and among unbelievers.

This is not always true, of course. Some men are able to labor from home with little exposure to the world. As a pastor, I have always considered it a distinct blessing to labor among God's people and to labor from home. Some men establish businesses of their own and are able to hire other believers as their workforce. This, in turn, means that some men labor in a Christian workplace among other believers—a blessing that ought not to be taken for granted!

But the vast majority of believers labor in places where ungodly men and women are in positions of authority and work alongside them. This reality cannot be avoided. But, as we have noted, neither should it be avoided. We are called to be a witness in the workplace too. That we are called to labor alongside unbelievers in the workplace becomes clear from the instruction we receive from God's word in this regard.

Several passages of Scripture address the employer/employee relationship. To understand them, however, we must appreciate the time and culture in which they were written. Although there were hired servants both in the Old and New Testaments (e.g., Lev. 25:40–53 and Luke 15:17–19), nevertheless, for the most part, there was slave labor. These slaves or servants had various positions. To some, more freedom was given than to others. But the relationship between one in a position of authority in labor and those who worked for them was that of master and servants.

Today in our free society, there is no longer master and slave in labor. It is employer and employee. The main difference is that when one is a slave to a master, he cannot quit his job and look for another elsewhere. In our society we have the freedom to do just that: if we do not like our job or our employer, we may quit and look elsewhere for work.

But the principles set forth by Scripture in the sphere of labor transcend time and culture. God's word is eternal in the heavens. What he commands in Scripture therefore holds true for the believer today too. Just as God has ordained the "powers that be" in the sphere of the home, the church, and government, so also does he ordain them in the sphere of labor. When the employer hires others to work for him, these employees are under his authority. That authority is granted by God. To state it plainly: *God* exercises his authority in the workplace by means of the employer. The employees, therefore, are subject to the authority of God as exercised through their employer. Such is the testimony of the Bible.

The calling of a believing employer is to recognize that his authority is derived from God, first of all. This stands in the foreground in Ephesians 6:9, "And, ye masters, do the same things unto them, forbearing threatening: knowing that your Master also is in heaven; neither is there respect of persons with him."

Employers are answerable to Jesus Christ, their Lord, in dealing with their employees. The employer must remember that Christ does not respect him more than those who work for him. He may not conduct himself in arrogance and pride in his rule over his employees, any more than elders may do so in the church of Jesus Christ. The employer must recognize that God has given him his position in the workplace. He must, in humble gratitude to God, conduct himself in a manner that reveals his love of God and the neighbor. This requires that as a servant of Christ, the employer must, with good will, deal with his employees as doing service to Christ, knowing whatever good he does to them, the same will he receive of his Lord (Eph. 6:6–8).

Furthermore, he must "forbear threatening." This does not mean discipline may not be administered by the employer. Wherever authority is properly exercised, so is discipline. If an employee is lazy or steals by purloining, proper discipline even to the point of firing him may be required.

But the employer must also show himself faithful, just, and kind in dealing with those whom he employs. He must pay his laborers enough to meet their needs, remembering that they too have families to support, perhaps tuition to pay for Christian education, and church budgets to fulfill. Paul says in Colossians 4:1, "Masters, give unto your servants that which is just and equal; knowing that ye also have a Master in heaven." Such is required of *every* employer, but those who belong to God's covenant especially understand how to deal with others as God has dealt with them.

The employee who lives in fellowship with God must likewise serve his Lord Jesus Christ in his dealings with his employer. Since God has given the employer authority over me in the realm of the workplace, the fifth commandment requires of me "that I show all honor, love, and faithfulness to my father and mother, and to all in authority over me; submit myself with due obedience to all their good instruction and correction, and also bear patiently with their infirmities, since it is God's will to govern us by their hand."[1]

This is Scriptural. God commands in Ephesians 6:5–7, "Servants, be obedient to them that are your masters according to the flesh, with fear and trembling, in singleness of your heart, as unto Christ; not with eye-service, as men-pleasers; but as the servants of Christ, doing the will of God from the heart; with good will doing service, as to the Lord, and not to men."

Now, all of this is good and well when our employer treats us justly and kindly, doing the will of God from the heart. There are many of us, however, that work for unbelieving employers. Some of these can be just and kind too, but many of them are unjust, demanding of us hard labor beyond our capacity or paying poor wages.

How are we called to react to such a contrary and harsh boss? I know how I would *want* to react! But then I am reminded by Paul in Galatians 5:16–17, "Walk in the Spirit, and ye shall not fulfil the lust of the flesh. For the flesh lusteth against the Spirit, and the Spirit against the flesh: and these are contrary the one to the other: *so that ye cannot do the things that ye would.*"

We receive God's instruction regarding that froward employer in 1 Peter 2:18–20,

> 18. Servants, be subject to your masters with all fear; not only to the good and gentle, but also to the froward.
> 19. For this is thankworthy, if a man for conscience toward God endure grief, suffering wrongfully.

1 Heidelberg Catechism Q&A 104, in Schaff, *Creeds of Christendom*, 3:345.

20. For what glory is it, if, when ye be buffeted for your faults, ye shall take it patiently? but if, when ye do well, and suffer for it, ye take it patiently, this is acceptable with God.

The servants or slaves of that day were not able to quit their job and go elsewhere when treated badly. At least today we have that freedom!

But it is here that a practical issue arises. In the late 1800s, when sweat shops and child labor were at their peak, labor unions began to form. These unions united the workforce together as a whole (organized labor) in order to coerce the employer to bend to certain demands made by the employees. By means of these unions the work place improved, wages were raised, and child labor was banished.

But though, from a human point of view, the unions were a force for good, nevertheless as they developed there were certain clauses put into place in the constitutions of these unions that are contrary to what we just learned in Scripture. One such clause is the strike clause. This clause became a major component in unions to force the employer to meet the demands of the union and the employees. If the employer did not meet the demands of the union, the union would instruct those who belonged to it to walk off their jobs, thus leaving their employer in difficult straits because he could no longer function without a workforce.

Such behavior on the part of the employee, however, is organized rebellion against the employer. Even when we might believe we are being slighted by our employer, God's word teaches us that we may not rebel. We may express to our employer that we believe he is doing wrong. But ultimately, we must submit to his decisions or leave his employ. The majority of unions have this strike clause. Therefore, membership in almost every union is a violation of the fifth commandment and displeasing to God.

Another important truth necessary to maintain in the workplace is that of the antithesis. The temptation is to view our fellow coworkers as a "workplace family," enjoying fellowship with them rather than with God's people. If our coworkers are themselves believers of like faith with us, then there is no problem—unless, of course, we spend more time with them than with our own wife and children.

The danger enters in, however, when we seek friendships with unbelieving coworkers outside of the workplace. This is a temptation because we spend a lot of time with them at work. We get to know them well. We share in common our work and even perhaps certain likes and dislikes. As a result, we can be drawn to them to the degree that we enjoy being with them after our day at work is finished.

This is common with unbelievers in the world. They search for fellowship with others that may share something in common with them. They may join a lodge or a gym, frequent a certain bar, socialize with neighbors, etc. The point is that a believer belongs to a family: the family of God. He ought to enjoy the fellowship of fellow saints in the church. That is where we find our family and friends—not the workplace.

This does not imply that we are not friendly with those with whom we work. We must be. We do share our work in common and we may talk with them about that work. We may share some laughs together. But always we let our light shine so they may see our faith. We are not spiritual recluses. But we ought never to allow them to take the place of our spiritual family of the church.

It is this type of mentality to which a labor union can also appeal. Labor unions often speak of themselves as brotherhoods. For example, the United Brotherhood of Carpenters or International Brotherhood of Teamsters, and so the list goes on. They appeal to their members as belonging to a special, illustrious fellowship of workers, to which they can devote themselves and in which they can find security together. Many of these same labor unions have a clause one must sign that swears allegiance to that union above any other institution—including a religious institution. Labor unions try to attract members by giving them a sense of belonging, a sense of family. In this too we may not be deceived. The believer does not belong to a brotherhood of men. He belongs to the brotherhood of saints. This brotherhood he is commanded to love (1 Pet. 2:17).

Life in the Covenant

As God's people who represent his cause and kingdom in this world, we rejoice in the fellowship we share with God, his Son, and his people. Work is a necessity for life in this world. We labor, and we labor *hard* to the glory of God and for the welfare of our families and church. Then our labors will reflect the place God has given us in his covenant.

—

Chapter 17

Subjection to Rulers

We live in the last days. In these days, perilous times will come for the church. As the antichristian world power develops, those in government will slowly strip the faithful church of its right to worship and preach the truth. Christians who insist on living according to the precepts of God's word will also be ostracized by society, and their individual rights will be taken from them by the government. We see it happening already today. The believer who belongs to God's kingdom in this world must therefore know his calling toward civil magistrates and governors.

Every believer has a dual citizenship. Everyone without exception belongs to an earthly nation. He is therefore under the rule of a government, whether that government be a dictatorship, democracy, communism (socialism), monarchy, or something else. God places us, as citizens of these nations, under the rule and authority of those who govern us.

On the other hand, we who belong to God's covenant and church are citizens of God's kingdom in this world. God is our divine Ruler who, in his sovereignty, reigns over all the kingdoms and nations of this earth. Under God, our Savior Jesus Christ rules. He sits at God's right hand in heaven and rules over all things on behalf of God himself.

The difference between these two kingdoms is that the kingdom of God does not come to manifestation in a kingdom on earth with national or geographical boundaries. God's kingdom extends from sea to utmost sea. It is a spiritual kingdom that is established in the hearts of elect believers. The earthly nations in which we are citizens are limited to the realm of the earthly.

We owe our allegiance to both kingdoms. In the United States, we pledge allegiance to the flag of the United States of America. God has placed us, either by birth or by immigration, under the rule of the magistrates in our land. At the same time, our full allegiance is to God and his Son and the spiritual kingdom of which we are a part. We are pilgrims and strangers in the earth, dwelling in a foreign land of sin and longing for the homeland in heaven.

Most of the time in our land, our dual citizenship does not contradict itself. Most of the time, we can freely live as citizens of God's kingdom within the earthly kingdom in which we dwell. But it has happened in the past and will happen again in the future that earthly rulers defy their heavenly Ruler, passing laws to which we as citizens of God kingdom cannot and may not conform ourselves. What then is our calling with respect to the earthly nation and its rulers in which we are citizens? To answer this question, we must examine our place as members of God's covenant and kingdom within the earthly realms in which we reside.

The Bible is clear that the powers or authorities that rule in our nation are given their position by God. Romans 13:1 states, "There is no power but of God: the powers that be are ordained of God." The teaching of God's word here is that all power (this word means authority) belongs to God. There is no authority in this world apart from him. He as Creator sovereignly rules over all the creatures of his hands—including man.

All men—including the rulers of this world— are subject to God's sovereign authority over all. We sing in Psalm 2:10–12, "Be wise now therefore, O ye kings: be instructed, ye judges of the earth. Serve the Lord with fear, and rejoice with trembling. Kiss the Son, lest he be angry, and ye perish from the way, when his wrath is kindled but a little. Blessed are all they that put their trust in him." Kings and rulers are subject to the rule of God and to his commandments.

At the same time, however, Romans 13:1 teaches us that those who rule in the various nations of this world are given their position of rule and authority by God himself. The powers that be are ordained of God. God has placed over the citizens of each nation their government and its magistrates in order to exercise *his* authority over us. God rules over us through those rulers he has placed over us.

It is wrong, therefore, to resist these rulers. Paul continues to write in Romans 13:2, "Whosoever therefore resisteth the power, resisteth the ordinance of God: and they that resist shall receive to themselves damnation."

Those in authority over us in government are "ministers of God." That may be difficult for those who have lived all their lives in freedom to remember when they now see those freedoms slowly taken away by those in government. We who are citizens of God's kingdom and covenant are called to bend the knee to those who rule over us in the earthly nations to which we belong.

As citizens of the earthly nation to which we belong, we must obey the laws of the land. We must be honest and live at peace in the society in which God has placed us. We are given this command in 1 Peter 2:13–15, "Submit yourselves to every ordinance of man for the Lord's sake: whether it be to the king, as supreme; Or unto governors, as unto them that are sent by him for the punishment of evildoers, and for the praise of them that do well. For so is the will of God, that with well doing ye may put to silence the ignorance of foolish men."

When the society and nation of which we are a part looks upon the citizens of God's kingdom with contempt, our honest conduct and faithful adherence to the laws of the land puts to silence the ignorance of foolish men. We obey the rulers God has placed over us by subjecting ourselves willingly under their rule and submitting ourselves to authority.

This same Peter who gives us this wise instruction, when called before the Sanhedrin and told no longer to preach the gospel, refused to obey those in authority over him. Was not he violating the very word of God he writes for the church? Not at all! The Sanhedrin was violating their calling before God. These elders of Israel demanded of the apostles that which was contrary to the will of their sovereign King in heaven. Peter was under obligation to obey God rather than men. It was by Christ's command that the apostles preached the gospel. They were heeding the command of the Ruler of their kingdom.

When secular rulers demand that their citizens disobey God, then the believer must bow first of all before the rule of God over them. Here is the rub, so to speak. Often in the history of this world secular rulers, in their attempt to break out from under the rule of God (Ps. 2), pass laws that demand that their citizens obey them rather than God. Those law-abiding citizens of their realm, in whom God has worked by his grace, must refuse to obey such laws.

But is that not rebellion? Obedience to God and his word is never rebellion. The believer may not *obey* the wicked mandates of men in government, but they must ever *submit* to the rule of their magistrates. The church does not take up arms against their government. The church does not rally its forces to do battle with the secular government. That would be rebellion.

Peter and the apostles did not rally the three thousand believers in Jerusalem in insurrection against their leaders. The apostles submitted to the punishment the Sanhedrin leveled against them. They were willing to go to prison for the sake of the gospel they preached. They rejoiced in that they were counted worthy of suffering for the sake of Christ.

The church is never militaristic in the sphere of the secular. This is the example Christ left for us when judged by the secular authorities. "Jesus answered, My kingdom is not of this world: if my kingdom were of this world, then would my servants fight, that I should not be delivered to the Jews: but now is my kingdom not from hence" (John 18:36). The kingdom of heaven is a spiritual kingdom that cannot be won by earthly warfare.

This truth is important for the church of Jesus Christ today. The true church of Jesus Christ today has come face to face with the scorn and ridicule of the godless society in which we live. In certain nations, many experience this even more than we do in our present country.

As the end of time approaches, the Bible clearly teaches that the antichristian kingdom will develop. As its name suggests, it will be anti-Christian—not in the sense that all Christians will be pressed out of society, but those Christians who live in godliness and take seriously the truths of Scripture. Not only will society at large despise them, but the government of this world will openly stand against them.

This antagonism toward the church of Christ is already evident in laws passed to protect those who walk in sin. For example, laws are leveled against those who refuse to support sexual immorality. Laws protect, and even support, mothers who abort (murder) their unborn children. In the United States, where freedom of speech and of religion were exercised as constitutional rights, these amendments are in danger of being circumvented by law makers. In many eastern nations, Christianity has always been repressed.

As the end of time approaches, the true church of Jesus Christ will become more and more "as a cottage in a vineyard, as a lodge in a garden of cucumbers, as a besieged city" (Isa. 1:8). Jesus warns his church in Matthew 10:18–20, "And ye shall be brought before governors and kings for my sake, for a testimony against them and the Gentiles. But when they deliver you up, take no thought how or what ye shall speak: for it shall be given you in that same hour what ye shall speak. For it is not ye that speak, but the Spirit of your Father which speaketh in you."

I know some say that this was a word spoken by Jesus specifically to his disciples and not for the church in latter times. But that is far too simplistic of an interpretation of this word of God. God's saints have often in history been called before judges and governors to be tried for their faith. What Jesus forewarns us about cannot be applied only to Jesus' disciples. It is a word to the church throughout the entire new dispensation, and therefore a warning to the church especially in the last days. These days are coming! The governments and godless societies in which God's people find themselves will no longer tolerate true Christianity. Tribulation approaches. We feel its tremors. How ought we to react to this?

Certainly we must always obey God rather than men. But that will entail persecution. Our reaction to this persecution by the government must always be that of humble submission. We may not rebel. Will this be difficult? Oh yes, it will! To see loved ones put in prison as if they are criminals. To witness Social Services remove our children from our homes because we are brainwashing them in the doctrines according to godliness. These will be real trials of our faith, comparable to the trials of God's saints in the Old Testament recorded for us in Hebrews 11. But God's word gives us great comfort in these trials.

First, Jesus tells us that when we are called before judges and governors of this world to testify against their sins, we need not fear what we will say. It will be given us in that same hour what we will speak, for it is not you or I that speak, but the Spirit of our Father that speaks in us. We must simply trust. God will take our part and give us the necessary strength to stand in these dread days.

Second, God's word teaches us in 1 Corinthians 10:13, "There hath no temptation taken you but such as is common to man: but God is faithful, who will not suffer you to be tempted above that ye are able; but will with the temptation also make a way to escape, that ye may be able to bear it."

God will never send us a trial in this life that is too great for us to bear. The work of God's grace in us is powerful. It upholds the faltering feet and makes the weak securely stand. We need not fear that we will stumble. We simply trust. After all, God is our heavenly Father who keeps his promises. In our hour of deepest need, he will not forsake us. He will be there with his strong right hand of righteousness. Underneath are the everlasting arms of God. We are the people of his covenant and kingdom in this world—a kingdom that will prevail.

The theme of Christ's sermon on the mount is the kingdom of

heaven and its righteousness. Upon the citizens of God's kingdom Christ pronounces this blessing in Matthew 5:11–12, "Blessed are ye, when men shall revile you, and persecute you, and shall say all manner of evil against you falsely, for my sake. Rejoice, and be exceeding glad: for great is your reward in heaven: for so persecuted they the prophets which were before you." As the citizens of the kingdom of heaven who are called to stand in submission to the magistrates of this world, even when they may persecute us for Christ's sake, we have this final word of encouragement: great is your reward in heaven!

—

Chapter 18

A Place for Entertainment?

What place does entertainment have in the life of the child of God? Between work and the busyness of home and family is there even room for entertainment in this life? What place does entertainment have in a family of God's covenant?

A true examination of ourselves in this area of our lives takes some sincere introspection. We say this, of course, because our flesh is drawn to the escapism of entertainment. Those outside of God's fellowship are restless, unhappy, and in many cases downright miserable. They do not have the peace that comes with salvation. As a result, unbelievers seek out any type of temporal fix they can find to make them happy. Some indulge in the base pleasures of life such as sexual immorality, drunkenness, and drugs. Others find ways of releasing their anger and passion through horrific music and unbridled dance.

The Bible condemns the sin of rioting (1 Pet. 2:13; Prov. 28:7), a squandering of one's money on pleasure or luxurious living. God's word also condemns the sin of revelry (1 Pet. 4:3). This term refers to the drunken, loud partying of lewd men and women that usually takes place in the darkness of the night. This entertainment found in the wicked world is used to escape the misery of sin and to find some kind of joy and peace in a world that is without God.

These forms of entertainment have no place in the life of those who belong to God's covenant. Paul lists them among the works of the flesh in Galatians 5 with the no-compromise statement: "they which do such things shall not inherit the kingdom of God" (v. 21). Peter says: "For *the time past of our life* may suffice us to have wrought the will of the Gentiles, when we walked in lasciviousness, lusts, excess of wine, revelings, banquetings, and abominable idolatries" (1 Pet. 4:3).

This type of entertainment belongs to the life of unbelief from which the child of God has been delivered. Those who walk in the sins we have just described stand under God's judgment and must repent and turn from these sins. Nor may young men and women of the church deceive themselves into thinking that such sins are allowable for a time in their youth. These are never proper means of entertainment that may be enjoyed by one who is a believer.

In every society that enjoys a certain measure of wealth and comfort, people become obsessed with every form of entertainment available. People live for fun. If something is not fun it is not worth a person's time. Most of a person's hard-earned money is spent on entertainment. People carry their entertainment in their pocket and with every spare moment are engrossed in it. People plan their day, their week, their *life* around it. Even worship services in many churches center on some form of entertainment: music, drama, testimonials, and humor. God forbid that people would have to sit beneath a long exposition of the word of God!

That being said, there is a place for legitimate entertainment in the life of a believer. Certain forms of entertainment are not necessarily sinful in themselves. Sports, picnics, social gatherings, vacations, restaurants, camping, *some* computer (or smartphone) games and social media are a few examples of this type of entertainment. These things we may enjoy in this life.

Solomon passes on these words of wisdom to us in Ecclesiastes 3:12–13, "I know that there is no good in them [the things of this life], but for a man to rejoice, and to do good in his life. And also that every man should eat and drink, and enjoy the good of all his labor, it is the gift of God." Or again in chapter 5:18, "Behold that which I have seen: it is good and comely for one to eat and to drink, and to enjoy the good of all his labor that he taketh under the sun all the days of his life, which God giveth him: for it is his portion."

Solomon practiced this too. We learn in Ecclesiastes 2 that he enjoyed wine (v. 3), built houses, planted vineyards, gardens and orchards (vv. 4–5). He had beautiful pools of water among groves of trees (v. 6) men and women singers, and musical instruments of all sorts (v. 8). But he concludes his quest for entertainment with these sobering words in verses 10 and 11: "And whatsoever mine eyes desired I kept not from them, I withheld not my heart from any joy; for my heart rejoiced in all my labor: and this was my portion of all my labor. Then I looked on all the works that my hands had wrought, and on the labor that I had labored to do: and, behold, all was vanity and vexation of spirit, and there was no profit under the sun."

When entertainment becomes the joy of our lives rather than a life of fellowship with our Father, it becomes vain and empty, resulting in restlessness, agitation, and distress in life. This is why it is important that we heed the instruction of God's word in 1 Timothy 4:4–5, "For every creature of God is good, and nothing to be refused, if it be received with thanksgiving: For it is sanctified by the word of God and prayer."

The various forms of legitimate entertainment belong to the area of Christian liberty. God has distributed to some more in the way of wealth than others. It is not wrong for them to pursue, let's say, a vacation that may be more extravagant than another might take. It is not wrong for them to buy and enjoy a boat that another might not be able to afford. One person may choose to enjoy one form of recreation and another a different form. We must be careful not to judge another according to our own standards in this area of liberty. Each of us will be held accountable before God in the area of recreation.

Several warnings are necessary, to which a believer must take heed in the area of entertainment.

First, the believer must be careful to distinguish between what violates God's law and what is acceptable to God. Life within the covenant precludes any recreation that violates what God teaches us in his word. We must take into account, therefore, what we have already learned in the chapters on God's law and the life of the antithesis that must characterize us.

This also limits the type of entertainment we enjoy. There are types of entertainment available in the wicked world that are aimed at *teaching* those who enjoy them. While a person immerses himself or herself in them for the simple purpose of having fun, Satan together with wicked men and women have a sinister motive behind them. They desire to inculcate into the hearts and minds of those who enjoy them the godless goals and principles—and even sins—of unbelief.

The chief forms of entertainment today are ungodly music and the movies. Those who sing and produce movies are intent on teaching us something in them. They have done a very good job of it today too! Satan has infiltrated the rank and file of the church of Jesus Christ and has begun eating away at the spiritual lives of young people and children in every way! So much so that the prevailing sin of the church today is a lack of holy living.

The songs of today croon about fornication, drunkenness, violence, hatred of God and his precepts. The sirens of this world lure us into their underwater lair of the inherent goodness and power of humanity. This world wants to find its way without God. And when we begin to sing along with them, they drown us in the lusts of the flesh and ungodly desires of this world.

The movies glamorize every sin from fornication to killing. Actors take God's name in vain, openly defying him, challenging his existence, and replacing him with superhuman men and women. How many children in the church believe that there was an age in which dinosaurs and prehistoric man ruled the earth? Evolution, the breakdown of the family, homosexuality, and adultery are brazenly taught to our children and young people in the movies—and now, also acceptance of the LGBTQ+ movement.

All the while, our children and youth—and we with them—are being taught, much of it through feelings, to be a part of this world of sin rather than a peculiar people and a royal priesthood unto the God whom we love. As a professor of mine once asked, "Why should we as God's people dig around in the trash cans of this world for our entertainment?" Yet, these forms of entertainment have become commonplace in the church. Will it mean the death of us?

A second warning is that the believer must not make fun and pleasure his *goal* in life. This too is an easy sin into which we can fall. We live in a land of plenty. We have almost anything that money can buy. When losing ourselves in entertainment, we lose sight of our place in God's covenant. The causes of God's kingdom begin to lack. We are quicker to lay a $20 dollar tip on a restaurant table after an expensive meal than to throw $20 in the collection plate on the Lord's day.

At times, because of our obsession with recreation, we become poor stewards of what God has provided for us. Tuition goes unpaid, the church budget is ignored, credit cards are charged to their limit—all because of our desire for high living. When this sin characterizes us, we become so drunk with the pleasures of this life that the hope for the life to come grows dim. We no longer look for Christ's coming. We no longer are willing to suffer loss for Christ's sake.

A final warning that must be issued is that entertainment must not push aside the home and family. We wrote of this a few chapters ago, but again we must emphasize it. The common trend in the church is to work and play. We spend hours at work in a day in order to earn enough money to eat up the rest of the day entertaining ourselves. There is no time left for family prayer and the reading of God's word with each other. Sporting events, going places with our friends, television, and going out to eat are but a few examples of recreational activities that are not wrong in themselves, but that can keep us so busy that we do not have time to sit down and converse together with each other as husband and wife or parents and children.

Is there a place for entertainment or recreation in the life of God's people? Of course! Some of this is even good for the believer. He too needs time to rest and relax. He may enjoy the fruit of his labors. Yet we must heed the wise counsel of Scripture in Philippians 4:5, "Let your moderation be known unto all men. The Lord is at hand." Let's seek first the kingdom of God and his righteousness. This will lead us into a sanctified use of entertainment.

Conclusion

Seeking Our Eternal Home

Heaven. We are pilgrims and strangers in this world who are passing through, traveling to our long home in the heavens. This is the place of our hopes and desires. Heaven is our home. Our hearts thrill when we sing the words of Psalter number 32, stanza 4:

When I in righteousness at last
Thy glorious face shall see,
when all the weary night is past,
and I awake with Thee to view
the glories that abide, then,
then I shall be satisfied.[1]

For the child of God who experiences the blessed fellowship of his heavenly Father in this life, death is not so harsh an enemy. More than once, I have experienced at the bedside of one who is dying the sigh of one longing to leave this life to go home. I sat by the bed of an elderly saint who insisted that I sing several Psalter numbers with him. Forty-five minutes later the Lord took him home to glory.

Heaven is where our Father lives. At his side is joy forever more. We will sup around the table he sets for his children there, together with Jesus Christ and our brothers and sisters. All our longings and

1 No. 32:4, in *The Psalter.*

desires will be satisfied there. We can fully appreciate why David would sing in Psalm 27:4, "One thing have I desired of the Lord, that will I seek after; that I may dwell in the house of the Lord all the days of my life, to behold the beauty of the Lord, and to enquire in his temple."

This is true because heaven is the place where the covenant of God with his people is brought to its perfect end. Heaven is the goal of God's covenant with us. It is that place where God's covenant is finally and fully fulfilled. How perfect is God's plan for all things!

Here is a recap. In himself, God is a covenant God. He carries on a perfect life of fellowship within his own divine being. In eternity, he chose in his plan to share that covenant life with a people chosen in Christ unto eternal life. God therefore created man with a mind and will, endowing him with the virtues of righteousness, holiness, and a true knowledge of him. By virtue of this creation, Adam and Eve shared in a life of perfect bliss walking and talking with God in Paradise.

But God had in store a much higher form of fellowship with his elect people than a mere earthly paradise. According to God's plan, man fell into sin in order that God might send a Mediator of a better covenant. During the Old Testament, God dwelt among his people in the tabernacle and later in the temple. But when Christ was born into the world, he was our Immanuel—God with Us. Through Christ's death, God's elect people enter into much closer communion with God. The Spirit of Christ dwells within them. By faith they are grafted into the very body of Christ. Yet, perfect, unmarred fellowship with God is not ours until we reach heaven.

Who can begin to describe what it will be like to walk with God in perfection without sin? John sees a beautiful vision of heaven in Revelation 21:3–4,

> 3. And I heard a great voice out of heaven saying, Behold, the tabernacle of God is with men, and he will dwell with them, and they shall be his people, and God himself shall be with them, and be their God.

4. And God shall wipe away all tears from their eyes; and there shall be no more death, neither sorrow, nor crying, neither shall there be any more pain: for the former things are passed away.

Indeed, this will be joy unspeakable and full of glory! While we are in this life there is toil, sorrow, restlessness, and hurt. Restless and weary we sigh. Afflictions, broken relationships, strife, and the threat of persecution remind us that this world is not our home. How many tears we shed in our lifetime!

Think of it! All these former things will pass away! They will be no more. The work of our salvation will be brought to its perfect end. There will be no more sin. We will not *be able* to sin anymore. Our hearts, thoughts, and desires will be completely pure and holy. Our glorified bodies will become immortal, sinless, powerful, and spiritual.

With the disappearance of sin, death, our last enemy, will be conquered. In its place, life forevermore. No earthly kingdom can provide us with this promise.

Then add one more item to this list: no more enemies! Those who opposed the cause of Jesus Christ in this world will be no more! Those who hated us without a cause, those who mocked God's people for their faith, those responsible for the blood of the martyrs will receive their just reward in utter desolation. The church will be free of these foes. Revelation 21:27 says, "And there shall in no wise enter into it anything that defileth, neither whatsoever worketh abomination, or maketh a lie: but they which are written in the Lamb's book of life." That too, no earthly kingdom can fulfill.

Ah yes: the beauty, joy and peace of heaven! "If heaven is not my home, then, Lord, what will I do?"[2]

One motivating principle ought to guide us as we live consciously within the sphere of God's covenant: the hope of eternal life. We can become so busy with our earthly lives at times that this hope wanes.

---

2 Albert E. Brumley, "This World Is Not My Home" (https://hymnary.org/hymn/HHOF1980/311).

The wealth and comforts of this life can possess our souls to such a degree that we seldom think of our heavenly home. We need to be reminded constantly of the glory that awaits us in the life to come in order that our hope does not fade away.

When the thought of heaven is held before us, we begin to sift through the clutter of this life, and our path here becomes plain. We are citizens of that kingdom of heaven. This world is not our home. This is not the place of our hopes and dreams. There is no comparison between life in this sin-cursed world and life in heavenly bliss.

When our goals are set on heaven, the things of this life indeed fade to the background. With patience, we wait for the life that is to come. We long for heaven. We anxiously anticipate a whole new life of perfection in a realm where the glory of our heavenly Father and the Lamb are the light of it. There is nothing better than dwelling with that Father who has chosen us and adopted us to be his own with an infinite love. Our sights are set on life with God's saints and Jesus Christ.

The Bible has much to say about our longing for heaven in its relation to our life within the covenant. First, there are several commands of Scripture based on our hope for the life to come. For example, the apostle writes in 1 John 3:2–3, "Beloved, now are we the sons of God, and it doth not yet appear what we shall be: but we know that, when he shall appear, we shall be like him; for we shall see him as he is. And every man that hath this hope in him purifieth himself, even as he is pure." God's sanctified saints are called to walk in purity in the hope that Christ will appear and we shall be like him. Our lives must be godly while we live in this world of darkness (see also Titus 2:11–13).

Another example is found in 1 Peter 3:15, "But sanctify the Lord God in your hearts: and be ready always to give an answer to every man that asketh you a reason of the hope that is in you with meekness and fear." Our hope becomes the basis for a sanctified life within the covenant. When others see this hope in us by means of our holy life, they will ask us about it. We then can be witnesses to them of that hope in us.

But our longing for heaven also gives us incentive to push on in this life when the going gets tough. The writer speaks of hope in these terms in Hebrews 6:19, "Which hope we have as an anchor of the soul, both sure and steadfast." When troubles surround us, our hope for the life that is to come serves as an anchor that holds steadfast in the solid ground that is Jesus Christ. The billows of sorrow and pain can beat upon us, but our hope in the coming of Jesus Christ is sure.

While speaking of the surety of the promise of God's covenant, the writer to the Hebrews reminds the people of that covenant, so that "by two immutable things, in which it was impossible for God to lie, we might have a strong consolation, who have fled for refuge to lay hold upon the hope set before us" (Heb. 6:18). What comfort is ours in this present valley of tears to know that heaven awaits us!

God's covenant is the rich heritage of the Reformed believer. To live apart from God is death. To live in fellowship with God is life. Life within God's covenant lends purpose to our lives. When we are old and our eyes grow dim, when the years draw nigh when we will say, "I have no pleasure in them" (Eccl. 12:1), may we be able to confess with Paul, "I have fought a good fight, I have finished my course, I have kept the faith: Henceforth there is laid up for me a crown of righteousness, which the Lord, the righteous judge, shall give me at that day: and not to me only, but unto all them also that love his appearing" (2 Tim. 4:7–8).

God's covenant of grace is with us in Christ. How could we live without its assurance?

In sweet communion, Lord, with thee,
I constantly abide.
My hand thou holdest in thine own
To keep me near thy side.[3]

What blessedness is ours!

3 No. 203:1, in *The Psalter.*

The Fruit of the Spirit of Jesus Christ
by Richard J. Smit

This beautiful paperback is the perfect gift book for anyone, young or old. This book discusses the nine aspects of the fruit of the Spirit (found in Galatians 5:22, 23) that proceed from that fountain, Christ, and which by his Spirit he works in his saints. The book encourages branches of believers and their seed unto a life of good fruit-bearing.

—

rfpa.org
mail@rfpa.org
616-457-5970

When You Pray Scripture's Teaching on Prayer

by Herman Hanko

The author tells the specific benefits of praying to the sovereign God of the universe, who knows our sins and weaknesses but loves us still. Valuable is the professor's clear explanation of how God can be likened to the father of an earthly family, loving and caring for his own dear children. If you have found your devotional life to be frequently barren, reading what the author has learned the hard way—over fifty years in the ministry—will not discourage you further, but will give you a renewed desire to fellowship with your Father in prayer.

—

Living Joyfully in Marriage:
Reflecting the Relationship of Christ and the Church
by Steven Key

Every Christian's relationship to Jesus Christ is pictured in the institution of marriage. Using the biblical principles behind this institution, the author provides sound instruction to each one of us on the relationship we have with Christ, our head, and with other members of Christ's church, the body. Practical instruction on topics such as right communication within marriage and in the church, the biblical roles of husband and of wife, and the calling to walk in the Spirit, will encourage Christians of every station and calling to live joyfully as members of Christ's body.

—

—

All books available at **rfpa.org**,
or by calling the Reformed Free Publishing Association
at **616-457-5970** or emailing **mail@rfpa.org.**

Our Mission

To glorify God by making accessible to the broadest possible audience material that testifies to the truth of Scripture as understood and developed in the Reformed tradition.

Reformed Free Publishing Association
1894 Georgetown Center Drive
Jenison, MI 49428-7137
Website: rfpa.org
E-mail: mail@rfpa.org
Phone: 616-457-5970